# How Did I Get Here? A Story of God's Grace

Janice Lucas

Copyright © 2021 Janice Lucas

All rights reserved. Printed in the United States of America. No part of this book may be used or reproduced in any manner whatsoever without written permission except in the case of brief quotations embodied in critical articles or reviews.

ISBN: 978-0-578-99591-5

First Edition: 2021

Published by Kingdom Promise Publishing LLC

Conyers, Georgia

www.kingdompromisepublishing.com

# Dedication

This book is dedicated to my heartbeats. The beautiful people on this earth who gave me more strength than they will ever know. I love you with everything I am.

# Table of Contents

Introduction ................................................................. 1

**CHAPTER 1**

The Beginning ............................................................. 3

**CHAPTER 2**

Hey Baby Girl! ........................................................... 13

**CHAPTER 3**

But Is He Prince Charming Tho? ............................. 21

**CHAPTER 4**

Starting Over ............................................................ 26

**CHAPTER 5**

God I'm Here!! ......................................................... 31

**CHAPTER 6**

Time to Relocate ...................................................... 44

**CHAPTER 7**

Saying Goodbye ....................................................... 53

**CHAPTER 8**

Is This One Prince Charming? I Know He's No Boaz ☹ ............ 60

**CHAPTER 9**

July 2012 .................................................................................. 66

**CHAPTER 10**

Pieces of Evidence: This is a true story after all! ............................ 73

**CHAPTER 11**

What Does It All Mean? Lessons Learned! ..................................... 79

# Introduction

All sorts of thoughts were running through my mind as I drove the forty minutes home from church that night. The ride was quiet since I dropped the kids off with their dad earlier, and I had just dropped my godson off to his parents. I could barely concentrate enough to drive. But that prayer tonight. I just received the most intense prayer by my spiritual mother that I have ever received. What did she see? What was she covering me from? My kids are healthy, I'm healthy as far as I know, but my marriage is horrible. We don't agree on anything! Everything I raised my children to believe in as a Christian family is now thrown out the window because of this man I allowed back into my life. He's verbally and psychologically abusive. What was I thinking!

The house was dark as I pulled into the driveway. I guess I got home first because I didn't see his car anywhere. I parked in the garage, waited in my SUV until the garage closed behind me. I grabbed my purse and the few items I stopped by the store to pick up, got out of my truck and closed the door. Everything was so quiet as I opened the door to the house. As soon as my hand left the doorknob and I turned to walk to the kitchen, a slender female figure stood just a few feet in front of me and BANG! A loud gunshot rung out and I knew I was hit. Then she lowered her aim and BANG! Another shot. While still standing, I threw myself against the stairs. She then grabbed me by my ankles and drug my body into the formal living room, behind the kitchen. My feet laid toward the door which led to the backyard and my head was towards the entrance of the room. I heard her shoes against the hard wood floor as she walked away from me. I could hear her picking up my purse, and the store bag I had when I came in the house. Oh God! What do I do God! God, please don't let me die like this! I hear her coming back down the hall to me. Don't breathe! Don't Breathe! DON'T BREATHE!

As I slowly opened my eyes, I immediately felt something very tight on my face, covering my nose and my mouth, forcing air into me. My throat and mouth were so dry. My body felt so heavy. I felt like I couldn't move. I looked around to see a white board in front of me with words and names I couldn't make out. A very large machine to the left of me, with something white that looked like a filter going up and down. My arm and wrist were sore, I tried to raise them and was barely able, but I saw the IV lines and medical tape. Surrounding me were all kinds of machines and tubes attached to different parts of my body. I thought she was coming to finish the job. I thought she was coming back to kill me. But my God, I'm still ALIVE!

# *Chapter 1*

# The Beginning

As a young girl, I didn't receive the attention or the time I would have liked from my mother. Mom worked 12 hours on the C-shift and had to arrive at work by 3:00 pm which seemed like every day. Her weekends and days off were consumed with men and partying. I was sometimes included but was more of a third wheel which always made me feel awkward. My Aunt, my mother's youngest sister, was my daily caregiver. We all lived in my grandparents' big farmhouse in upstate NY with other family members. There was me, 3 cousins, their mother (my mother's sister), my mother's second oldest brother, my caregiver, and my grandparents. My aunt was only about sixteen-years-old when she started caring for my 3 cousins and me. Many times, she didn't have any money or food to feed us after we came home from elementary school or on weekends. We were taught to collect cans and bottles because the local grocery store would take them in exchange for money. We would walk the 2.3 miles to and from the grocery store just so we could eat. I knew that my family didn't have much money, but what they did have was a lot of love, closeness, and stability. I was closest to my grandmother; she was my all-time best friend! Grandma was loving, assertive, and sassy! She even taught me how to do the electric slide in the middle of the kitchen floor!

I was used to not seeing my mother, but one day, it was odd that I hadn't seen her for several days in a row. I asked grandma where my mother was, grandma said "she moved out". I couldn't believe what I heard! Moved out? Where could she have possibly gone? Grandma told me that my mother had left me there with her and moved out to be with the man she was dating. Something in my stomach sank. I felt like someone had just dropped a boulder into my stomach and left it there. Why would she leave me? I knew we didn't have the typical mother daughter relationship, but to leave me? I asked if I could talk to my mother, grandma called her on the phone, handed me the receiver, I said hello, and mom sounded like she was surprised to hear my voice. When I asked if I could come see her, she said yes. Later that afternoon, I got dressed, trying to look my best, then grandma drove us to the city of Rochester to visit my mother. Although we had more family in Rochester, I never really went into the city much. As we left grandma's house in the suburbs, it was funny how the further we drove into the city, the more the houses changed, and the neighborhoods started to look different. Instead of green, manicured lawns, I was now looking at houses with front yards full of dirt instead of grass and houses with boarded windows and guys sitting outside laughing and talking. We finally pulled up to a light green house with a metal fence around the front yard. My grandma told me my mother was inside. She motioned for me to go to the house, telling me it would be ok. I was scared as I got out of the comfort and safety of her car, closed the door, walked around to the sidewalk, opened the gate and closed it behind me. No one was outside, and I had butterflies as I walked up to the unknown door. There was no doorbell, so I knocked lightly but no one came. I knocked again a little louder, and an older black lady answered. She smiled at me and asked me to come inside. The house was darker than outside, but I could still see all the faces. Some kids were there who looked to be about the same age as me. And there were what seemed like a lot of adults. About four adults were sitting around the kitchen table laughing loudly and drinking, and a few more standing by them. The kids were in the living room with several women. I guess their mothers watching after them. Everyone said "Hi", they all seemed nice. The lady told me my mother was upstairs and to go see her.

I climbed the dark staircase to a second floor. The house smelled old, like cigarettes, and some other smell I didn't recognize. As I slowly walked down the hall of the second floor, there were several rooms that had open doors. I didn't know which one she was in. I cautiously looked into each room, but she wasn't there. Then I came to a door on the left of the hallway that was closed. I knocked on the door and could hear her voice on the other side telling me to come in. Mom was in a house dress looking like she was ready for bed when I opened the door. The next thing I noticed was my mother's large stomach! Mom was short like me and had always been a petite curvy woman. She never had a big stomach. This is when mom told me that she was pregnant and having a son. I was an only child for twelve-years, then my baby brother came along.

About a year and four-months later, my mother moved me from my home full of relatives, love, and stability, into an empty, inner-city apartment with a newborn baby sister, a toddler baby brother, and their father whom I had met years ago when I was nine-years- old. He used to take me fishing with his nephews and because I never knew my real father, I trusted and looked up to him to be a father figure in my life.

Mom's future husband had a good job and was revered by his family and friends. Yet, he had an alcohol problem that no one else seemed to know or care about. Plus, he preyed on young girls; including me and my cousin. We never knew anything about our own fathers, and we thought having a father-figure was a dream come true. One night when I was about eleven-years-old, I woke up to the voice of my aunt yelling. My two aunts and my mother were chasing my future stepfather around the house. They were cussing and yelling at him about how could he touch her (my older cousin). They finally chased him out of the house. It was quiet. Very eerie and quiet until I heard a loud "CRACK" from outside and my aunt screaming in pain. Somewhere along the way, he found a 2x4 and was hiding at the corner of the front porch and surprised my aunt when she came near him. He broke her ribs that night and left with the police. My cousin and I are just two that I know of; if there were others, that was a secret he took to his grave.

After a few years went by, I learned to spend my nights with my bedroom door locked. I always felt as if I had to look over my shoulder at all times and was afraid of what might happen if my door didn't stay locked. He would say little sly comments when I would walk by. When I was a little older, I would hear light knocking on my door. At first, I could not figure out what it was. Then one night I went to look and when I opened the door he was standing on the other side, looking surprised that I opened it. I immediately slammed the door, locked it, and ran back to my room in fear!

After that night, I continued to hear light knocking on my door (he didn't want to wake my mother), then the door handle would jiggle violently. And on the nights my baby brother would have nightmares, I prayed that he wouldn't hear me sneak quietly downstairs, or whisper to my brother. I would lay in my brother's bed to rock and comfort him back to sleep. One night as I cradled my brother, I drifted off to sleep until I felt this hand running up my thigh to the top of the blanket where my stepfather pulled the blanket off of me. I was half asleep and it took me completely by surprise. I jumped and rolled over to see who was touching me. I opened my eyes wide, and stared directly into his eyes, and for some reason it startled him or woke him up to what he was doing, and he ran run out of the room. I lived in constant fear of what he might try to do to me and would try to stay out to avoid being home with him. My mother never kept tabs of me, where I was going, who I was with, or what I was doing. But I was my siblings only caregiver and felt guilty for not being at home with them. So, one day after not being able to take it anymore, I told my mother what had been happening. I was afraid of what my mother might say, and how she would handle it. I hesitantly told my mother that her husband had tried to make advances towards me and enter my bedroom at night. Mom looked at me like I was crazy! A look that said, "How dare you lie about something like this"? Mom said she would talk to him. I just walked away thinking something wasn't quite right. A few days later mom called me to the living room. I could see my mother and stepfather sitting where I was headed, they were talking quietly. Mom made me sit by my stepfather and repeat everything I had told her, so he could hear my accusations. But mom took his side. How could she? After being sexually abused herself as a young person, how could she not take me seriously? I was a good girl (for the most part), never got in trouble, kept good grades, never lied about important things or anything I was asked about. How could mom not trust me? Was this man more important to her than I was? I walked away completely heartbroken. I knew our relationship was not good, but I never imagined my mother would side with the enemy. I guess the past should have told me different, but I could not see it then. And to make matters worse, someone told his family members everything that happened! They cursed at me and ostracized me for what they heard I had said. At just thirteen-years old, my world had fallen drastically, and I never thought it could get any worse.

Between my stepfather's drinking and violent mood swings, and my mother's drinking and drug use, my young siblings had no one to care for them. No one else in my family helped. No one in their father's family helped. Maybe they didn't know about our struggle; maybe they had their own issues to deal with. I never knew why, but I did know my mother's motto: "What happens in this house, stays in this house". I was never allowed to talk about the happenings of the house with anyone that didn't live there.

I started working as a babysitter at fourteen-years-old to make enough money to take care of my siblings. The money I earned helped me pay for their clothes, diapers, wipes, and food. I bought all the food in the house and paid the only bill not covered by social services, the cable bill. I babysat, kept the house, and fixed anything that wound up broken.

I was broken. I never really understood that I was broken until I reached adulthood, but even at a young age, I just knew there was a sadness that I could not shake. I would not be able to fix my own brokenness. At fourteen-years-old I smoked weed, drank alcohol, and started having unprotected sex with guys that made me feel special. I wanted to feel loved and accepted. That is what was really missing, love and acceptance, but I was not able to put a name to it until much later in life. I was lied to about the identity of my father. I was given the name of a man whom my mother had dated, and my last name was his last name; but he was not my father. I could not understand why mom just would not be honest with me; or was she, herself broken despite her best efforts? No matter what, I could not seem to have the relationship I desired from mom.

One day I came home from school to find mom angry, high, and drunk. I knew immediately from the way her mouth was twisted to one side when she spoke and from how badly she slurred her words. Her eyes were like ice daggers. I could not think of what I may have done wrong. Mom told me I had to start giving her money for rent to live there. Now I was raised old school by my youngest aunt and grandmother, never disrespect your elders, always do what you're told, and you never talk back. But that day something stood up inside of me and I told mom no! I was already raising her children and paying household bills. Isn't that enough, I thought to myself! But mom had so much fury in her eyes from my answer, she leaped and grabbed me by the throat. We both fell to the floor. I felt the weight of my mother's body while she choked and screamed at me, she yelled all kinds of obscene names, calling me lazy and worthless. As I lay under my mother, I was struggling, crying in disbelief, and kicking to get free. After a few minutes, my mother's boyfriend (yup...you read it right, boyfriend) came home, ran to the struggle, and picked my mother up off of me. Shaking and in tears, I ran upstairs to my attic bedroom, locked the door behind me, sat on my bed and cried. I could not believe my mother hated me so much! I held the heart necklace in my hand as I thought about how much of a lie it was. It was literally the only thing my mother had given me that was worth something. Mom gave it to me as a symbol of the love we shared. The necklace now meant nothing to me. I snatched it off my scratched and bruised neck, opened a window, and threw it out into the snow. The cold air was brisk as it hit me in the face, but I barely felt it through my broken heart. The necklace was never seen again.

I closed the window and walked back to my bed. Not a few minutes later, my best friend Gwen pulled up and honked the horn. I was not expecting anyone, so I ignored the noise at first. But the honking didn't stop. I finally got up, wiped my face, and went to the window to see what was going on. An intense feeling of release came over me when I saw my friend. The one person on the entire earth I could confide in that didn't judge or look down on me. I opened the attic window, "Come on already let's go," my friend yelled up to me. I grabbed nothing but my keys and ran down the stairs and out the door to the safety of my friend's car. Once inside, Gwen immediately could tell something was seriously wrong. She asked, "What happened to you?" I urged my friend to "just drive" with my head down. As we started on our way across town, I shared in detail play by play of everything that happened that day and the tears flowed again. Gwen was angry. My heart was hurt more than it was angry. When we arrived at Gwen's house, we immediately shared what happened with Gwen's mother. "Mommy", as the household members called her, told me that I could stay with them for as long as I needed. Overtime, Mommy sat me down on many occasions to share with me the characteristics of a real woman.

What she looked like, how she speaks, how she behaves, how she handles bad things that happen in life, and how she can't do everything alone. I learned so many things from Mommy while I lived there, like how to make wise choices, and what it means to have respect for yourself. She was more of a mother to me than my own mother had ever been. I learned how a mother sacrifices for her children. I learned how a mother puts her children first. Life lessons that helped to mold me into the woman I would become. Mommy also spent time ministering and encouraging my mother through her addiction, through her depression, woman to woman without me ever knowing.

For the next two years I stayed with family and friends who became family. All the time I was away from home, my mother never called to speak with me or send money to help with my care, food, or supplies I may have needed. But in reality, I never expected her to. All of my belongings came from Goodwill, and trust, I was made fun of and bullied at school because of it. I was super shy, had lower than low self-esteem, and was terrified of people and what they thought of me. I guess being this introverted caused me to be labeled a snob. Other kids assumed I thought I was better than them. In reality, I just wanted to go to school and be invisible.

Years ago, when I was a young girl still living at my grandparents' house, I was rummaging through some stuff and somehow came across some old letters my mother had written when she was a teenager. The letters seemed like they were more like diary entries that really had no intended reader. They talked about what my mother was going through, her emotions and feelings about life. Then I found a letter written while mom was pregnant with me. It talked about the fears and uncertainties she was feeling. And it also said she had a doctor's appointment to end the pregnancy, and that it was unwanted. That I was unwanted. I knew my relationship with my mother was not what I saw my friends have with their mothers, but I never could have imagined that my mother never wanted me and worst of all, made plans to end my life. I was shocked! I was hurt! I could not believe what I had read. And I never told anyone of finding that letter. During the two years of living with others off and on, all of the memories came flooding back to me, and in my mind, it made perfect sense of why my mother never checked on me. She never wanted me from the start, and now that I was gone, she could live her life without what she didn't want; me.

I missed my siblings terribly. When I finally did see my mother again, to say the meeting was awkward was a serious understatement. My Aunt Sue arranged the meeting in attempts to bring us back together as a family. I never received an apology, but I also felt bad for leaving my siblings in my mother's care. I agreed to go back home, without paying rent, and that way I could keep an eye on my brother and sister. Once back, I could see that the household situation was different. The house was clean, including the kids' room. Someone must have paid the bills because everything was on and working. And mom appeared to go longer between her high and drunken binges. She was actually teaching my brother how to ride his bike and taking the kids to the park down the street. She even started working. It appeared that somehow mom had decided to put her life back together. And the stepfather was nowhere to be seen. I asked where he was, "he lives somewhere else" was the answer mom gave. I felt safe being there. Joy and laughter were a part of the house and it felt like home.

Mom was better on the outside but still broken and hurting on the inside. I never knew about my mom's pain or what taking the drugs were numbing her from. One winter day as I stood by the kitchen window, I watched as my downstairs neighbor was walking with someone, but their head was covered with something red, and I was unable to make out who it was until they walked up to my door. It was my mother! The red thing covering her was a white shirt drenched with her blood! The neighbor dropped my mother in my arms and called 911 explaining what happened. She had been locked in an apartment with her boyfriend, who was one of the neighborhoods biggest drug dealers, and stood 6'7" where my mother was only 5'1". He beat her with cinder blocks, a clothes iron, his fists, his steel toe boots, and any other thing he could lay his hands on. The ambulance arrived and I went to emergency with her. I talked to mom the whole way trying to keep her awake as tears streamed down my face. Despite everything, I loved my mother, and it was breaking me inside to watch her like this. Once in the hospital, I watched the doctors stitch up a massive gash on my mother's scalp from where she was hit with the iron. This was the first time I had ever seen so much blood and flesh at the same time. I held my mother's hand the entire time, but I could not muster any words to say. I sat by my mother's side as they bandaged and iced her where needed. Why? Why would mom put herself in a situation to be hurt like this? Were the drugs worth it? Why didn't she mention his name when the hospital personnel and the police asked her who did this to her? I never understood, all I could do is take mom home, and take care of her until she recovered. Next thing I knew, the boyfriend and my mom made up and it was like nothing ever happened. WHAT! How could you possibly forgive and forget what he did to you? I still could not understand, but little did I know my mother was teaching me some very bad life lessons that I would unknowingly repeat.

# Chapter 2

# Hey Baby Girl!

When I was seventeen years old, one of my grandmother's sisters, Aunt Bernie, moved close to where we lived, less than a ten-minute walk from my house. I was overly excited to be able to visit family as much as I wanted. Aunt Bernie was always welcoming and full of love and hugs whenever I visited. And there were so many cousins that lived with Aunt Bernie. Some adults, others were teenagers around my age, and some of the kids were younger, but they were all family.

During one of the trips to Aunt Bernie's house, I ran into a friend, one of the guys that lived in the neighborhood. We would walk together, joke, laugh, and just talk about the happenings of life. At this point we had known each other for a few years, and always kept it friendly. This particular trip around the corner, my friend was walking with another guy. He was incredibly handsome and well built. I felt butterflies the very first time he looked at me. He and I immediately noticed one another and then my friend introduced us. That was the day I met Trenton. From that day on, Trenton and I were inseparable. We laughed, played, and genuinely enjoyed each other's company. I fell head over heels very quickly and believed he felt the same. After all, he told me he loved me.

After about four months of dating, I noticed that I missed my period, which was very strange because it was always on time. One day I joked about being pregnant, and Trenton picked up my small frame, laughed and spun me around and kissed me with complete joy and love in his eyes. When I told him it was just a joke, his face dropped, and he was sad but laughed along. When I realized this time it was not a joke, I called Trenton to come over so I could tell him the amazing news. This time he did not have a look of love or joy, this time it was sheer disappointment. All of my past transgressions had caught up with me. Someone told Trenton about my attempts at finding love in all the wrong places and Trenton changed the way he looked at me. I was no longer the one he wanted to share his time with, I was the neighborhood whore, the neighborhood slut, and he made it very clear where he stood. He told me to have an abortion and he would not be in this baby's life or have anything to do with me. He called me every name in the book. How could he not see me for who I really was? He was just like the rest, only wanting one thing from me. I was crushed and cried for days before telling my family I was pregnant and was keeping the baby.

My pregnancy journey was not an easy one. I graduated early from high school and walked the stage to get my diploma at four months pregnant. My dress was a size 0. No one could tell I was carrying a child, and no one at my school knew that I was pregnant. I decided early on that my child would have everything she needed. I worked three jobs during my pregnancy, moved out of my mother's apartment and found my own. I was leaving my old life behind, preparing for a new one with my precious daughter. I was eager and ready for this new beginning; the possibility of having an amazing future with my baby girl was overwhelmingly joyful. Trenton even told one of his cousins about our relationship, and that I was carrying his child. Her name was Tonya and she reached out to me regularly during my pregnancy.

I loved my little one-bedroom apartment. I felt free, safe, and secure for the first time in a very long time. I loved that I was the only person living there, and that I was the one who made all the rules. The used couch from my grandmother's house came to live with me in my living room. I found many yard-sale gems to decorate with; my daughter's crib being one of them. The crib was made of cherry wood, practically brand new and stunning! I only needed to purchase new bedding to go with it. I was as prepared as I could have been doing it on my own. No baby shower, no gifts or presents from my family. I truly felt like the black sheep of the family and that it was my own fault. Promiscuous, leaving home early, teen pregnancy, no other family member my age was doing any of those things. I felt like there was something wrong with me. My self-esteem had always been low. I thought I was just ugly and scrawny. Besides, if my own mother didn't want me, why would someone else? Alone at night, are the times I would get very lonely, but by living this new life, I felt like I was getting a second chance to be a different person.

One day, the landlady of the apartment complex introduced me to the handyman who lived a few apartments up the hall. His name was Jacob. He was sixteen-years my senior, light skinned (which was a turn off), and always seemed to wear the same sweatpants every day. Definitely not appealing! I was not in the least bit attracted to him. But he seemed like he was a decent person. He would come down and ask for a cup of sugar or flour every once and a while, obviously trying to flirt, but it didn't faze me in the least.

Everything seemed to be going well until one day I decided to go on a date with some new guy. Yup, a date while pregnant. While out, I slipped during a round of miniature golf and fell. I certainly had no business trying to find comfort or companionship while carrying another man's child. But again, I was still trying to find the love and acceptance I so desperately longed for. There was no pain at the time of the fall, but the next day my water broke. I was only twenty-nine weeks pregnant, way too early to try to have this baby! I was calm yet cautious. "Ok little one, it's too early; just stay inside and stay healthy." I was telling this to myself as I drove across town from my apartment to pick up mom, then across town in the opposite direction to the hospital to check myself in. Due to having a slow leak of amniotic fluid, the doctors stopped the contractions and decided to keep me in the hospital until the baby came naturally. Now although I always felt very alone, I had a huge family. My grandmother had thirteen children. At the time, nine were still living. My great-grandmother had double digit kids, and great-great-grandma had a bunch too. Some lived in Georgia where grandma was from and some had moved to Rochester. Since I grew up around all of my family, there were days they would come and visit me in the hospital. Uncle Raymond would bring a bucket of Kentucky Fried Chicken with sides each week. I was so happy for the food because the cafeteria stopped serving food at 7pm every day. How could they do that to a floor full of pregnant women? Anyway, the main goal was to focus on the instructions of the doctor to keep my baby safe and healthy. I only walked, when necessary, I ate as I needed, and those lovely steroid injections in each butt cheek weekly were given to help the baby's lungs develop because they knew she would come early.

At thirty-three weeks pregnant, I started having really bad back pain. I thought it was from sitting in bed for so long, and apparently my nurse thought the same thing. All day my nurse brought me a pink hospital chuck. She drenched it in water, then rung it out, and microwaved it to be used as a heating pad. The heat helped somewhat until it didn't any longer. This was about the time the nurse decided to check to see if I was actually in labor and sure enough, I was! The first person I called was my mom, then I called my Aunt Dorothy, and the last call I made was to Tonya. My mom and aunt came to the hospital as quickly as they could to help me in the delivery room. I was calm but anxious, more afraid of not knowing what to expect, all coupled with extreme labor pains. After just a few pushes my little miracle was born. All of the anxiety, worry, and pain just vanished into thin air until I noticed my miracle was born without any color! She was just as light and bright as she could be! Head full of hair, but not brown skinned like her mother or her father. Now for some of you who don't know, not all black babies are born with color, some of them develop color along the way. I sure didn't know! My mom and aunt were both there and didn't say anything! I screamed, "What's wrong with my baby, what's wrong with her? Why doesn't she have any color? Is she sick? What's wrong with her?" Then, the doctor came over to assure me that the baby was fine, a little jaundice and underweight, and that some black babies develop their color over time. Really? I had to hear that from the doctor when I had two family members with me? Just another day in the family.

My precious baby girl was born on a perfect Friday the 13th, at four pounds and one ounce. The doctor believed that if she had come full term, she would have been born at a normal healthy weight. She was able to breathe on her own, but again she was too small. She was placed in the (Neonatal Intensive Care Unit) NICU until the jaundice went away. She was able to nurse immediately and always had a great appetite!

Being in the hospital for such a long time before baby girl was born caused me to lose the jobs I had. I had to turn to social services to take care of our needs. Now in NY back in the day, social services (or welfare) paid out enough to cover the cost of rent and electric, and you were normally given food stamps to use for groceries. I was also getting WIC benefits which helped to supply me with healthy food to eat during my pregnancy and while nursing baby girl. However, I had no extra money for food at the hospital or gas for the car. The baby stayed in the NICU for four weeks. I nursed her around the clock and usually took naps while with her in the hospital. Overnight was when baby girl slept the longest and I used this time to go home, shower, eat, change clothes and return to the hospital before little mama woke for her next feeding. With all the back and forth I was doing, my neighbor Jacob noticed and asked what I was doing out so late so often. He said it was not good for a young girl to be out so late on her own. Really? "What are you my dad now", I thought? I explained about my daughter and what happened. He said, "Well since we live in the same building and I get off work around the same time, why don't you page me, I'll come pick you up from the hospital, and bring you back home". He briefly went inside of his apartment, ripped off a piece of paper, wrote his beeper number on it and handed it to me when he came back to the door. To a young girl with zero dollars, that sounded like a great plan. I could save what little money I did have for gas or other necessities like baby diapers and wipes! So that was our agreement. For the next 3 weeks, whenever I was ready to leave the hospital, Jacob would get a page and he would pick me up. The first night he picked me up, I was standing inside not far from the main hospital doors, and I heard a faint sound of music with some serious bass, obviously coming from a nearby vehicle. "That's him," I thought. Sure enough, as the car pulled in front of the hospital, his music was blaring until I walked up to the car. We chatted about each other's day during that first ride back to the apartment. Initially I just went home, then after a few nights Jacob said he had something to show me in his apartment. Now I had never been inside of his place before and was kind of hesitant about going in, but he didn't have to take the time out to help me so maybe it was ok.

When I went inside, the smell of food hit me like a ton of bricks! I had barely eaten anything all day and was famished! The smell of the food was almost intoxicating. Jacob told me that he cooked an amazing meal just for me. There was smothered pork chops with green beans and butter beans, mashed potatoes with homemade gravy, a homemade cake for dessert, fruit, and what looked like homemade iced tea. It all looked divine! I was so surprised that someone would look out for me like that! Who is this guy that would feed me? Take me to and from the hospital so I can take care of my daughter and not worry about gas money. It had been a few weeks of getting to know him and he had not tried to sleep with me, so why would he do this? What was up his sleeve? No one would do all of this just because. These were the thoughts swirling around in my mind. After all, he had to have a motive, right? Everyone else did. After eating, and thanking him for his generosity, I went back to my apartment to shower, nap, and change clothes.

This ritual continued for about two- weeks, then one night Jacob also had a bath drawn for me along with another amazing meal. I ate dinner, bathed alone, put his clothes on, and went down to my apartment to take care of the rest. During dinner, we talked about life, my life, his life, his previous relationships, my previous relationships, his children, my child, and I felt like maybe this is what a real relationship is like. Maybe this is what it is like to be with someone who genuinely cares about you and looks out for you. Someone you can be completely open and honest with. Could he possibly be the one to love me for the rest of my life?

The beautiful day came when I was able to bring baby girl home. I was so excited to have my daughter all to myself! No more doctors and nurses telling me how much time I could spend with her. My daughter was the absolute joy of my life. She was beautifully brown, head full of gorgeous curly locs, and the sweetest temperament of any child. She was truly a blessing. While I was in the hospital, I made a vow to myself to be the best mother I could possibly be. I had no problem denying myself of my needs, what mattered most was that my daughter had everything she needed or wanted. This included her mother's love, time, and energy. I did everything in my power to be all of those things for her.

As I was rushing down the hall with my hands full of all baby girls' things from the hospital, her baby bag, and baby girl in her car seat, I knocked on Jacob's door as I passed by. I was inside of my apartment for a whole five- minutes before Jacob was at my door asking to see baby girl. He swooned over her and it was quite possibly at that moment I fell in love with him. Over the next few weeks, baby girl and I spent a lot of time with Jacob in his apartment.

Jacob had a way of talking that made me feel at ease. The conversation was easy, I felt like he actually listened to what I had to say, that he really cared about what was going in my life. I felt he not only cared for me, but that he truly cared for, and even loved my baby girl. In my eyes, we felt like a real family. A new, immature, growing family. He opened up about his past. We talked about how he was just one year clean from doing cocaine, he shared all the things he did for drugs, the people he used, how he manipulated his family and friends. I just assumed it was due to the drugs, never would have imagined what I would have to confront it in the very near future.

# Chapter 3

# But Is He Prince Charming Tho?

Jacob and I became a couple and spent all of our time together. I was so in love with everything that was happening in my life. I didn't have to go back to work because Jacob took care of me and my daughter, I didn't have to bother cooking because Jacob loved to do it, and I didn't have to keep the house by myself because he enjoyed helping. I thought I had found my prince charming. But I could see some things starting to change in Jacob. He would go out and not come home around the time he said he would. At times he refused to answer his pager and I would worry about his safety. And whenever I wanted to be around my family Jacob always had some kind of issue. He wanted to know who was going to be there, whose house I was going to, the exact time I would be home, and everywhere I went I had no choice but to take my daughter with me. Initially I didn't mind, because at the end of the day my daughter did not belong to Jacob and I was very protective of her. Slowly his behavior and attitude towards me started to change. He had to know my every move and every place I was to be. If I went to work, I had to spend every break and lunch on the phone with him the entire time. His behavior became more controlling, but I didn't recognize it that way, I just thought he was in love with me and that was how he showed it. Two years went by and Jacob and I now had a daughter together. But the behavior only grew worse. I had to take both girls with me whenever I left the house. Jacob was very secretive about his comings and goings, and if I was visiting at his place, I was not allowed to answer his home phone or his house door. No matter what. While I was still in the hospital after giving birth to my second daughter, a nurse brought in paperwork to document her name and complete her birth certificate. Since I knew this was Jacob's child it was a no brainer for me to write his last name as the last name of our child. Jacob looked at me and actually asked, "Are you sure about this?" What? How dare he even tune his mouth up to ask such a ridiculous question. I was not allowed to be out of his eyesight without his permission. He even monitored me with my family.

One particular Sunday, Jacob had invited some of his friends to come over to watch the game. I was at his place with the girls cleaning and preparing for his guests. His house phone rang, and as instructed I didn't touch it. I figured it was probably just one of his friends calling about the game. But I was wrong. A soft female voice spoke on the other end saying that she missed him and could not wait to see him again. Wait . . . what? Without thinking I picked up the phone and said, "Hello, who is this?" The other woman explained who she was, and that Jacob was her man. That they had been dating for quite some time and she wanted to come over later that day. Hold up, wait a minute! So, you mean to tell me that this man, this controlling, manipulative man whom I love, is cheating on me? I was beyond furious. I went on to explain to her who I was, the mother of his child, and that I WAS HIS WOMAN! I was only twenty-years-old and the other woman sounded much older. The other woman simply laughed and said to have him call her. I immediately hung up. How disgusting and so disrespectful. I had never been cheated on and I didn't know what to do. I knew Jacob would be furious with me for answering his phone, but I just did not care. How dare he have me cleaning his house, getting his place ready for his friends to come over and be cheating on me at the same time. I looked at my girls who were at one point playing together on the floor, but now they just looked back at me. As my hand was on the phone receiver my mind immediately went back to watching my mother being abused and fighting with men. That memory made me calm down, pull myself together, and finish what I was doing. I would not be that in front of my girls!

My stomach was in knots. I paced back and forth anxiously anticipating Jacob's arrival. I was shaking as I tried to stay calm for my girls. But I also had a temper, I could really go off in the right situation. But I was more afraid than angry. All I could think about was how Jacob would react once he learned that not only did, I answer his phone, but that I also had a conversation with his other woman. Now, I shouldn't have been that concerned, after all he was the one in the wrong, I really didn't do anything any other woman in my shoes would not have done. But I knew my man. I knew that anything that happened would somehow turn around and made to be my fault. I knew about his temper, and I knew that in his mind he was never wrong, no matter what. And I also knew it didn't matter that the girls were there. His temper had no filter.

Not long after I finished getting everything ready for the game, I heard a car pull into the driveway. He's here. I tried to stay calm as Jacob was getting out of the car and walking up to the house, I could hear his keys jiggling in his hand as he unlocked the door to come inside. I looked at him and said, "Hey, how'd everything go?", he said everything went fine and greeted the girls. As he walked into the kitchen, he was pleased to see everything was together. The snacks were laid out, the cups and plates were ready for his guests to arrive. Then he looked at me he could tell something was not right. "What did you do?" he asked. I was shocked by his question. Not what's wrong, or what happened, but what did I do? So, I told him everything that happened, how he had some woman missing him, and the conversation she and I had. I was pissed and showed it. I did not hide my emotions. I talked to him with a long knife in my hand from prepping the snacks, wanting him to lie to me. I tried keeping my voice down because the girls were just in the next room, but he did not care. He screamed at me, "Didn't I tell you to never answer my phone, that's what you get for being nosey!" What! He didn't apologize. He didn't say the other woman lied. He didn't even try to explain himself. He didn't even try to come up with some kind of excuse to use. Before I knew it, Jacob had snatched the knife out of my hand, held the knife to my throat and told me that if I ever disrespected him like that again, it would be the end of me.

Once he let me go, I went straight to the girls, and packed them up in their stroller. I was trying to grab everything at once, so I didn't have to go back inside the house for anything. With tears streaming down my face, I tried to leave the house as fast as I could, but Jacob wouldn't let me leave! He rushed in front of me and tried blocking the door. I pleaded with him to let us go and to move out of the way. The girls just stared at us both. He finally moved and I was able to get out of the house. I immediately went to my car, but he popped the hood as I was trying to get the girls in the car, did something under the hood so it wouldn't start, all to try to stop me from leaving. Pissed and determined I took the girls out of the car, loaded them back up in the stroller and started walking to my apartment, when all of a sudden, I heard someone walking behind us. I had already crossed the busy main road, and he had crossed after me. Yelling obscenities, calling me out of my name, saying I was too weak to handle anything that came my way. He told me that I was not woman enough and that's why he needed to cheat. And he was loud! The further down the road I got, the more people were turning their heads to see what was going on.

I was twenty-years-old, scared, and in the worst relationship. I was shy and embarrassed. I was ashamed to be with someone who treated me so badly, but he was the father of my daughter. I knew what it was like to grow up without a father and I did not want that for my child. What was I supposed to do? So, I stopped walking, turned around and started walking towards Jacob. When Jacob saw me turn around, he then turned around and went back to his place. I followed, saying nothing else. We all went inside of the house. I stayed with the girls upstairs making sure they were calm and ok while Jacob was downstairs entertaining his friends. Once the game was over, and all of his friends had left. Jacob allowed me to take the girls home. We never talked about that day again.

   I didn't want Jacob to leave my girls. From that day on, I tried my best to be obedient to his commands. I never wanted him to have a knife to my throat again. But that did not stop his anger, or his abusive ways. One day I wanted to leave his place, but he didn't want me to leave. He picked me up while we were outside and slammed my 115lb frame onto the ground. There were many times that I ended up with bruises, scratches, or worst of all, emotional and psychological wounds that people just could not see. After a year and a half of this abusive behavior I could not take it anymore. I was done. I didn't care what he thought or what he would do if I left. My children deserved better and I deserved better. I left Jacob, moved into an apartment on my own with just my beautiful girls. I thought Jacob would just leave me alone, but I was wrong.

# *Chapter 4*

# **Starting Over**

For the next year and a half, I spent every waking moment looking over my shoulder. Paranoia and anxiety were normal emotions throughout my day. In one downstairs apartment where my girls and I lived, Jacob circled the entire place, banging on every door and window until the police showed up, and then would repeat the same behavior once they left. Bang! Bang! Bang! Bang! Bang! Hour after hour after hour. I would call the police to make him go away, but he would hide or disappear as soon as they showed up. Then the police would leave with no resolve. The banging would keep the girls awake all night long. He did not care about the kids, nor did he care about me. He just wanted to have his way. It was like some sick game for him. He got pleasure out of torturing us. He wanted the family life, and the single life to whore around whenever he felt like it. But I meant what I said. I said I was done, and he was not allowed to see me or my girls.

One night my aunt convinced me to allow her to watch the girls so I could go out and breathe a little without any fear. I knew one of the most likely places I wouldn't run into Jacob was at a club. He did not like the club scene and never went. Once the girls and I were finally ready to leave, and not five minutes after we left the apartment, I heard an all too familiar voice. The voice called for me from a car which pulled up next to us as I was walking. Jacob must have been watching and waiting for us to leave the house. How else would he have known? I tried very hard to hurry the stroller along with the girls to my aunt's house. I wanted to be rid of Jacob and not worry about what he was saying or trying to do. As I kept ignoring him, he became more and more enraged. Just as I pushed the girls onto the other side of a driveway, Jacob swerved his car into the same driveway, and made me jump out of the way of his car. If I had not jumped out of the way, Jacob would have hit me and possibly injured the girls since my hands were firmly around their stroller.

I stood for a second shocked that he tried to hit me. The sound of the tires screeching on the pavement was all I could focus on. Then I ran as quick as I could to my aunt's house with the girls. Once I got there and told everyone what had just happened, they were surprised but not surprised at the same time. They all believed me because they had seen Jacob's temperament firsthand. But as with the many other times, no one did anything to help me.

The next time I moved, I made sure it was an upstairs apartment. No more stalking around my house and banging on my windows and doors, I thought to myself. But to my surprise, Jacob was still able to figure out a way to make life difficult. One particular night, after I put my girls to bed, I heard what sounded like scratching coming from my balcony window. Now there was literally no way anyone could get onto my balcony from outside except a very thin tree that ran from the downstairs neighbors' porch to my balcony. I doubt it would have been able to sustain my weight. It was just that tiny. Since Jacob weighed almost 100 pounds more than I did, I was not anticipating any problems. I peered from around the corner to look toward my window, and sure enough there he was. Right on my balcony, trying to pry his fingers into a small hole in the window screen. My house phone was in my bedroom, and I called 911 immediately. There was an empty lot on the corner of the street, so Jacob was able to see the police cruiser as soon as they turned the corner. Next thing I knew he jumped off the balcony. I ran to the balcony door, unlocked it, and tried to show the officers where he might be hiding. But again, they didn't find him and left. I stayed on the balcony for some time after that and saw him barely get up from his hiding place and limp through that empty lot to wherever he parked his car. Later I learned that he shattered his ankle that night and he needed a plate and some screws to fix it. He still has them to this day and the scar on his ankle to prove it.

My main goal was to keep me and my children safe from Jacob. I also needed to make a living to support my family, so I decided to go to school for Medical Office Administration. I didn't have my own car, so I rode six city buses a day to handle business. One bus to downtown, a second bus to drop my girls off to mom to babysit, a third bus to class, and then I did it all again at the end of the day to get home. My girls were my entire priority. For the first time in my life I was not thinking about dating. I was not concerned about having someone in my life to fill the void that was lingering. I only wanted to make sure my girls were taken care of and kept safe.

I met some really great people when I went back to school. One lady was an evangelist. At the time I did not really know what that meant, but I had heard the term before when I was younger and used to go to church with grandma. The evangelist had another friend who would become my friend. We would discuss faith-based issues, topics of religion, and spiritual relationships. I was able to relate to most of what the ladies talked about. I thought that as long as didn't sin I was good to go. I was never much of a curser, so foul language was never an issue for me. I always tried to treat people fairly and equally. I was honest, and I put my family first. I was celibate and not dating anyone; no booty calls . . . nothing! I didn't drink (much) and was not a smoker. I did try cigarettes to calm my nerves about Jacob but found smoking was not for me. Four months after starting, I quit and never picked them up again. When the ladies started talking about all the things that were pleasing in the sight of God, I felt like I was good. I was in there. As long as I was a good person and continued on in life the way I was living it, that was good enough. And when I said it out loud, the ladies laughed at me. I was so confused. I thought I was doing everything already to please God. The evangelist told me being a good person was not enough. No one gets to the Father but through Jesus Christ his Son. She quoted this scripture, "Jesus saith unto him, I am the way, the truth, and the life: no man cometh unto the Father, but by me," John 14:6. She went on to explain that we as believers at one time, were unable to come to the Father; however, because Jesus Christ sacrificed his life, eternal life was now possible. She told me we could come to the Father through Jesus Christ our Lord by first believing that Jesus Christ is our Lord and Savior. She went on to tell me, we must believe that Jesus died for our sins and then we would gain eternal life in Heaven.

HUH? So, everything I was doing was not good enough? I shifted my entire life around without even realizing it to become this person who was so close to being pleasing to God. Little did I know, God was cleaning me up and molding me into the woman He was calling me to be.

I could not shake the evangelist's words. I could not leave it alone. How could I not be living a life good enough to please God? How could I do more? The evangelist's words swirled around in my mind all night. I could not think of anything else. I was up late that night, long after the girls were put to bed, and I kneeled by the side of my bed, put my hands together and began to pray whatever came to me. "Father God I believe that you are God almighty who created the heavens and the earth. I believe that your son is Jesus Christ my Lord and Savior. God, I also know that I am a sinner and I pray on this night that you save me from my wickedness and forgive me for all of my sins. I pray that you come into my heart on this night and I will forever praise your Holy name. In Jesus mighty name I pray, Amen". That night by the side of my bed, I gave my life to Christ and slept better that night than I had in years.

The next day I was eager to see what had changed. I was eager to see what was different in life now that I was saved and was a Christian.

# *Chapter 5*

# God I'm Here!!

That next morning was pretty uneventful, but I was feeling so free! I had never experienced anything like it. As I got off the second bus, I was so excited to share with my friends what happened the night before. Unfortunately, I wouldn't see them until it was time for lunch. We were in the middle of the cafeteria when I explained everything I felt the day before, everything I did, and how I prayed to God! The evangelist was happy but not excited like I thought she would be. She reached her hand out to mine, I held it and next thing I knew the three of us were standing in the middle of the school cafeteria in a circle holding hands and praying. She led me in her version of the repentance prayer, and I repeated everything she told me to with fervor and passion. I had a new desire to give my life to Christ. I didn't care who was watching us. I didn't care what people would think or say. I just had a desire in my heart to be pleasing to God. When the prayer was over the three of us celebrated. I guess she wanted to make sure I was really saved. This part of my story is proof that God can and will meet your right where you are.

I didn't know any other ministry or church in Rochester outside of the one my grandma used to take me to, so I didn't really know where to go to be taught, to grow, or to be planted. The evangelist taught me the basics about the importance of having a spiritual covering and that I needed a home church to sow my tithe, time, and talent. She backed everything she taught me with scripture when we were together. I purchased my very first bible and started reading for myself and learning the Word of God. The first thing I noticed was how so many sayings or phrases I heard growing up, or that people used in regular conversation actually came from the Bible. There's nothing new under the sun. Treat people the way you want to be treated. What goes around comes around; all based out on scriptures. I bet most people never even knew that, but yet they criticize God and His words.

One day as I was walking to the bus stop, I happened to look up at a house I was walking pass, and I saw flames coming out of the attic window as if the house was actually on fire. It didn't startle me, I only wondered why I was seeing it. It was an open vision that God was giving me although I didn't understand what it meant, I know what I saw. It was so interesting how God started moving in my life. I made a full commitment to give my all because I learned that Jesus gave His all for me. I started hearing conversations, and my thoughts started to change. Not realizing it was God communicating with me. God knows that I absolutely love music and one thing that bothered me was that the only gospel music I heard was really old school gospel. Not quite my taste, but I thought that was the only option available to me. One day at my mother's house, a cd came in the mail, addressed to the wrong person. It was a gospel cd by Helen Baylor. Mom was going to throw it out, but I told her I would take it. I was so excited because I had never heard of this artist before and I desperately needed to listen to music that would uplift my mood. I did not realize it was my spirit that needed to be fed until I learned about that later. Her cd, all the music on it, lifted me in a way that I had never felt before. It was like I was in an entire zone anytime I played it. This cd was continuously on repeat for months and months at a time until I learned about some other artists. Artists with a more contemporary sound, artists that spoke to the pain and hurt buried in my heart that allowed me to cry out. When I cried out, I could feel the peace of God surround me. I was falling deeper and deeper in love with God. I literally felt like a brand new person. I wanted to shout it out from the mountain tops, but my family did not understand, and my friends definitely were not about that life.

One day, the evangelist was speaking at a local church and asked me to come support her. Of course, I would be there! When I showed up to the church a little early, I saw an older woman in the front yard of the church cleaning up the paper, bottles and other trash that had been thrown by passersby. She greeted me with kindness. I just thought maybe she was a mother of the church and didn't really think too much about it. I greeted her and she smiled back at me and said I was welcome to go inside and sit wherever I'd like. I started walking cautiously inside, went up the stairs to the sanctuary, found a seat and sat down.

There were some that greeted me as a visitor who seemed to be nice people. The first thing I noticed was other people there around my age and children around the same ages as my girls. A woman around my age started speaking at the pulpit and she welcomed everyone to the service. She prayed, read a scripture, and introduced the praise and worship team. Then they began to sing. I was in love! The music, the lyrics, the harmony, it was EVERYTHING! While they were singing, the older woman that was outside cleaning up, walked into the pulpit. I thought, "Oh, maybe she was going to do the announcements or maybe she was the pastor's wife, or something". How wrong I was. When praise and worship was over, she stood up and went straight to the podium and introduced herself as the pastor of the ministry. What, she was the pastor? I thought only men were pastors. Why would the pastor be out cleaning the yard? Didn't she have people to do that for her? What I learned was that she was a humble servant of God before she was a title. This was a HUGE lesson for me. I am a servant, always wanting to make sure those around me are being cared for. I was able to connect with the servant in her instantly. The pastor proceeded to introduce the evangelist and the evangelist took her position. She greeted the people, gave honor to the shepherd of the house (which I had no idea what that meant), and began preaching her message. The message was good, but that message was not the only thing I took with me that day. I wanted more. I wanted more of the music, more of the wisdom and I wanted to learn more from this humble female pastor. I found out about their weekly services and began visiting regularly until the church became my first church home. I joined with excitement, a hunger to learn as much as I could, and a zeal to be of service in every area that I could.

The church members were so welcoming, I felt as though I had made friends for life. I now had people, friends, that I could talk to about the Bible who were able to help me with its interpretations. More importantly how to hear for myself how God is speaking through his Word so I could then hear the interpretations for myself. People who showed me how to live a holy life, a consecrated life, a life free of fornication and adultery. I learned what faith was. How to have it. How to build it. How to walk in it. I gained so much spiritually and naturally from this ministry, but I also gained a family.

Unfortunately, not every experience was a pleasant one. God will show you the way, but it's up to you to follow. Although God was working in my life, bringing healing and deliverance, I was still broken. I was still making mistakes, despite what my spirit wanted. My spirit just wanted to please God. I just wanted Him to be pleased with who I was in Him and who I was becoming. There is a scripture, "Watch and pray, that ye enter not into temptation: the spirit indeed is willing, but the flesh is weak" (Matthew 26:41). I thought I was doing well in my prayer life, but I didn't know what to watch for. It is imperative to watch out for the tactics and devices that the enemy uses. The enemy's distractions in your walk will lead to open doors for sin to enter your life. Having a prayer life alone does not prevent you from walking in sin. The enemy, the devil, is real and he is cunning. He has a calling on his life as well. His entire goal is to walk through the earth seeing who he can devour (completely destroy). The enemy will use the smallest opening of doubt, fear, anxiety, stress, or sadness to sow the smallest seed in your thoughts that can grow into something larger which develops into sin. When you see the enemy, in any way, shape, or form, you have to use the power that dwells within us all , given by God to rebuke the enemy. This was a lesson I learned all too well. To rebuke the enemy is to turn back; to express strong disapproval; to come against.

Eventually after following me to church, attending the church, and finally joining my church, Jacob and I resumed our relationship and not long after we got married. My first mistake was not being honest with myself when we went to couples counseling. I was honoring him, and not sharing the reality of what our relationship was and my true concerns about the future. I felt that it was my job as a woman of God to only allow the good of the man I was with to be seen. I was holding him up and esteeming him as my husband before he had that right. My second mistake was I completely disregarded our past as if it never happened. Knowing all that he put not just me, but my daughters through, and I threw it right out the window thinking it was the past; that you're supposed to let go of the past in order to move on with your future. Which isn't completely wrong. However, if you have known someone for years and their behavior never changed while you were together, never changed when they were in their last relationship. They are saved, supposedly Holy Ghost filled, but still exhibited the same behaviors; those are all massive warning signs and red flags. Now don't get me wrong, there are plenty of people who, when they have allowed God to work on them and allow true deliverance to hit their lives, change and become better people. But for that to happen it takes time. Time, I did not allow. Changes I thought would happen immediately because I knew he had been saved before, while this was my first time. He had been married twice before and this was my first marriage. I thought because he had been down these roads before, he knew the ropes, he knew how this was supposed to go, and he would be able to teach and show me how it all works. Boy was I wrong. Loving someone alone can't bring about change. If you and/or the other person need to change, it is not; let me repeat, it is not your job to try to change the other person. Only God can bring the real change to you or to them. The key about change, not change that only lasts during a particular season, or for a particular event, or when people come into your life; real godly change has to be wanted. Real change has to be desired. The person who wants change has to be so hungry for it that they will do and give up anything in their life that comes against the possibility of them getting the change *(the deliverance)* they desire. I learned that I was still hurting and still broken from my younger years but I desired real deliverance in my life so I could be the best servant, wife, and mother I could be.

I dove right in! I dove into the Bible, not really knowing what to do with it or how to really read it, but I understood how important it was to read what God was saying to His people. This book was supposed to be our Biblical Instruction Before Leaving Earth (B.I.B.L.E). I also heard a lot about the Proverbs 31 woman. I didn't know about her, I just heard that we are supposed to be like her. But why? What made her so special over all the other women of the bible? I decided to research this woman. In the process of reading about her and how she conducted her life, God started putting thoughts into my head which I learned was revelation or understanding about what I was reading. This woman would wake up early in the morning before the rest of her household to go before God and pray. She would receive instruction from God about her day. She would hold her husband before God praying for his strength, clarity, instruction, and other things specific to her man. She would pray for her children and the rest of her family. She would also pray for other people, circumstances, and events. In praying for herself, she would seek God on the intimate areas she needed God to work on within her.

Back then, I heard how we as women should follow the man as he follows Christ because the husband is the head of the household. The problem is, if you don't know what Christ is saying, or how he is speaking to that man, how do you know to follow him? Since I didn't know, anything Jacob said I just went with it. "Don't wear makeup, real women of God don't show off by wearing makeup. Don't wear form fitting clothes, real women of God don't show any curves. Don't be too outspoken in mixed company, real women of God are always humble". Regardless of how the other women in ministry dressed or behaved, it seemed as if there was always a scripture to back up his comments. Jacob cheated and he was manipulative. With each wrong, he made his mistake my fault. I just went with it thinking that it was all a part of the role as his wife. I was living a life full of manipulation and mental abuse by him twisting the Word of God to suit his personal needs. I knew it didn't feel right nor did it seem right. Yet, whenever I would ask someone about it, I was always told that he was my husband and it was my job to serve him, please him, and maintain the peace in the home. One day I questioned Jacob in front of group of people, and there were both men and women present. I openly expressed my thoughts that were different from his and he immediately gave me this look like he was pissed that I opened my mouth. Things had been going well between us and I thought maybe my prayers for his temper and his abusive behavior to change were being answered. But it was my going along with his every whim that was keeping the peace. My cowering when he said anything and lowering my intelligence, my self-worth, my beliefs to appease him and keep the peace. There was no arguing over what he said or what he did. There was no debate. Later that night after we got home and I put the kids to bed, Jacob wanted to have sex. He hadn't said much since we left our friends and I was honestly afraid of what may happen next. A married woman does not withhold sex from her husband, so when he motioned that's what we were going to do, that's what we did. But he took his anger out on me in the bed.

He pushed himself inside of me so hard as to hurt and punish me for speaking out. He refused to stop despite my fighting against him until he finished his business then got up like nothing happened. The next morning, I stood in my bedroom, with my hands on my dresser in front of the mirror with my head down and I told God I can't take this anymore. I felt like no one loved me, no one cared about my well-being, that this world was better without me in it, and that my mother made a mistake by having me. I planned in my head who would take care of my children if I committed suicide. I would call into work and after dropping the kids off to my mother, I was going to come home, and I knew exactly how many pills I would take. I knew I was home alone, but just then I felt a hand on my left shoulder, I raised my head and saw a massive angel standing behind me and told me "Everything is going to be ok". I blinked and the angel was gone. I immediately felt the peace of God and never again did I consider suicide as an option. It took every bit of strength I had to tell people I trusted what was going on in my home. How I was being abused and how Jacob was still cheating. I was told that he was a man. That that's what men do. That it is my job to keep the peace in my home and eventually it will all turn around. I was told this by the elders of my church. This is not to bash the church or the counsel of those who have lived longer and experienced more. This is just to show that other people may be broken too and may not give proper or sound advice. Just because someone may hold a title in church doesn't mean they are not still human and have their own stuff to deal with. Eventually I learned that God wanted better for not only my life, but the lives of my children as well.

At twenty-two-years-old I became my own version of the Proverbs 31 woman. I repeated all the things that she did in my own way and God began giving me a certain peace even I could not understand. I had a certain kind of insight about my husband that was different. I had a different insight into my children and those around me. I stopped worrying about what Jacob was doing because God always revealed what He wanted me to know. Our family grew the second we got married and my first son was born. We lived in a house where his exes knew where he lived. They would come by to give me money to give to Jacob and walk away with nasty smirks on their faces. Whenever I asked about the visits and money, it was simply none of my business. One day Jacob told me that he never used to clean his house or pay his own bills, that these women would handle everything for him, but he never told me what they would get in return from him. I'm sure I knew whether he confirmed it or not. Eventually we moved. I don't know if any of them ever knew about our new location, but I never saw any of them again after that.

When my oldest daughter was four-years-old, during a time when Jacob and I were separated, she was not feeling well. I would take her to the doctor and would be told she just had a cold, or she just wasn't feeling well. One day they completed bloodwork. When the results came back abnormal her pediatrician wanted us to see a blood specialist (hematologist). After many blood tests, and many specialist visits, it was determined that my baby girl's immune system was fighting against her very own liver. She did not show any signs of jaundice. She would be tired, unable to play and barely had an appetite. I knew something was not right and this was certainly more than a cold. As parents we are our children's biggest advocates. We know our children better than anyone else (other than God) and it is our job to advocate for them. I had no medical background, I had no formal training, but I knew my child and I knew something was wrong.

After Jacob and I got married, baby girl was almost five-years-old when she had a stroke. God had her wake me up in the middle of the night telling me she had to use the bathroom. Now she was fully potty trained and knew to use the bathroom on her own. I told her to go to the bathroom. Then God had me get up to look in on her and I watched her lose her balance and saw her eyes move rapidly. I called to Jacob and told him we needed to take her to the emergency room. We stayed calm to keep her calm as we rushed her to emergency room. The drive was less than ten minutes away. By the time we arrived she began hallucinating. The staff worked quickly to start an evaluation and running tests. They also started administering medications for meningitis. I stayed by her side the entire time talking with her and trying to keep her mind with me. I stayed as calm as I could. After her spinal tap, and before the results came back, baby girl fell into a coma. I called out for the nurse, and next thing I knew they took her out of the emergency room to PICU. I immediately fell to the floor praying in tongues! I prayed for her safety and for her healing. I never thought about who would see me or what others might say. At some point Jacob was trying to pick me up from the floor. I stood up and went back into the area where we were. A lady who was with her child in the room across from us came to our room. She handed me a flower and told me she was praying with me for my daughters healing. As I told her thank you, I was completely blown away that a stranger would care about my child enough to pray for her and to tell me that she was praying. That to me was a sign that God heard my prayer, and that He was with us.

Because God had her wake me up and I was obedient to check on her, I believe my obedience saved my daughter's life that night. What if I had just rolled over and ignored the voice in my head to check on her? How different the outcome could have been for her. Baby girl had a long recovery, but God brought her through successfully. She started kindergarten on time just a few months after fighting for her life and she returned to her regular class. She was still going through physical, speech, and occupation therapies, and taking medications, but she was a fighter. She was strong and kind. She was loving, and she had a special relationship with God; which at the time I was unaware.

I learned how important it was not to just be a lay member, or a person who was simply a member of a ministry, but to be an active member of a ministry and to have your hands actively busy on the things of God. All of our children were also learning to be active church members. I was working ministry, Jacob was working ministry, and the kids ushered and sang in the children's choir. I felt like God was finally smiling down on our family, it seemed as though we were in a good place. Financially we were doing well. Life was peaceful and joyful. Nevertheless, a drastic change was coming. I would not be ready and never could have seen what was to come two years down the road.

Baby girl kept getting sick even after all her labs and non-evasive tests came by fine. Her immune system just kept attacking her liver as if it did not belong to her. She had all her original organs that she was born with and I had no history of this kind of illness in my family, so the doctors said they needed answers to make sure she was on the correct medications. This time, the doctor and staff did her wrong by not following protocol during the procedure. The doctor was only supposed to perform a simple biopsy of her liver to test the actual tissue and see what was really going on. Instead, he chose to perform the procedure trans-jugular (by inserting the biopsy tools into her jugular vein) instead of making an incision in her stomach. It was supposed to be less invasive and lead to a quicker recovery for her. We waited almost double the suggested time and were told that everything was fine. There were no complications. After the procedure she was sent to her hospital room even though she was supposed to be in recovery. She kept telling me she was hot, and I explained I could not open the hospital room window. She complained her stomach hurt. In my mind, I was thinking she should not be having stomach pain from a small biopsy, especially since there was no incision made. I tried consoling her as much as I could. After each complaint I told her nurse every complaint she had. The nurse continued to do nothing, until I was unable to wake up my Baby Girl! She was bleeding out from the procedure. We were then rushed out of her room and placed in a family waiting room in the hallway. By the time I heard "CODE BLUE" called out over the loudspeakers, I saw my beautiful daughter being rushed by with her stomach ballooned out as if she was five-months pregnant. She was bleeding internally. Some of the cleaning staff somehow knew who we were and came into the waiting room and told us that something wrong happened while she was in surgery.

By the time I was able to see Baby Girl again, she was in PICU fighting for her life. At seven-years-old she lost all of her motor function, vision, speech, ability to eat, and was incontinent. It took a week after they stopped giving her mediations to keep her in a coma before she opened her eyes on her own. It would be another few days before she could follow people with her eyes. More days to breathe on her own without the help of the ventilator. Another two weeks before she could smile again. The milestones were long and difficult. From making sounds, gaining enough strength to hold her head up on her own, to finally gaining the ability to swallow to eat. In all, it took about a year before she could almost sit up on her own.

In one fell swoop, our entire world was turned upside down. The once happy, smiling, singing daughter and big sister needed more care than we knew what to do with. Her baby sister was five-years-old and her brother was three. Neither of them could understand why sissy could not talk to them or play with them anymore. But we came together as a family to learn and provide for her every need. All I knew how to do was pray.

I am not a proponent of suing people. I genuinely believe that it is simply human nature to make mistakes. But to make a mistake of this size and to cost my daughter her livelihood without remorse or apology was not acceptable. A lawyer was sought out and his wife just happened to be a registered nurse who, once she heard the story, requested medical records almost instantly. Let's just say that at the end of our lawyers' investigation, the hospital, the doctor who performed the procedure, the nurse, and other staff were found negligent and even fined by the state. This started a very long legal battle to make sure Baby Girl would always have her medical and physical needs covered. I never wanted anything. My main goal was only to take care of my Baby Girl.

I encouraged Jacob to start his own business and I began working overnight so we had more flexibility for Baby Girl's specialist appointments, medical needs, and ability to take care of our other children. We were making decent money and was able to take care of our children. But then Jacob decided to stop paying bills. All of my money had to go to the bills and only if I ran short, he would pitch in. The money never came to my hands, but it would go directly to the service provider. He would do literally anything to make sure I had no freedom. Jacob was still up to his old tricks, lying and cheating his clients, flirting, and trying to have sex with them. One day when I was big and pregnant with our fourth child, a visitor from church told the pastor's daughter who was her friend, that Jacob was hired to do some work at her home and was leaving inappropriate voicemail messages on her answering machine. She saw that his family was with him and decided to share all that he had been doing. We had a meeting after church where he was confronted, admitted to everything but only after we listened to one of the messages. He was simply told to not do that again by leadership. I was upset and hurt but not surprised. The car ride home was full of "well this is what you get", "this is what happens when you want to know the truth", "are you happy now", "your pain is your own fault". Never once did he say his actions were wrong. My God, something needs to change, and it needs to change fast!

# Chapter 6

# Time to Relocate

After a few years, we uprooted our family and relocated to Central Florida, believing it to be a ministry move for Jacob. He was to submit himself and be mentored by an amazing Prophet of God. I felt like it was a good move. Although we had no family there, it was easier to push Baby Girl in her wheelchair since there was no snow or ice, the natural Florida sun was good for her liver health, and a new beginning was going to be just what our family needed, especially with all the infidelity and abuse that was a part of our story. I honestly believed that Jacob's behavior would change being under a strong man who treated his wife like a queen and showed his children love and guidance daily. I was hoping he would see how it was supposed to be done and become a better man and father. I thought him seeing firsthand what was possible would motivate him to be a better husband and father. His reasoning of not being better was always that no one showed him. But at the end of the day people only do what they want to do. You can either live life the way you've seen it lived, or live life the way you want to live it. We all have choices.

After getting settled in Central Florida, the physical abuse ended, but the emotional, psychological, and financial abuse never went away. Overtime I began to spend more time with the pastor's wife who was a true godsend send for me. She could see it all. I never had to say a word. She encouraged me to find me and love me again. She helped me to understand that it was not the will of

God to be treated the way the kids and I were being treated. She provided biblical principles and wisdom to guide me. She also taught me how to pray for my husband and really hold him up before God. How to anoint him without him knowing he's being anointed and how to go in my secret place and pull-down strongholds in his life and the lives of my babies. On the other hand, she was also realistic and told me like it was.

Now Jacob was always a money hungry, materialistic person. Early on in our relationship he shared with me some of the things he would do for money or the way he would get people, mostly women, to give him money. Somewhere along the way, I agreed that Jacob could adopt Baby Girl. I thought he loved her, but the day the adoption was finalized, instead of turning to me, the mother of this child, he turned to the attorney and gave him a big hug with a smile and walked with him down the hall. I knew it didn't seem right at the time, and immediately it made me very nervous. A few years later, the judge finally awarded Baby Girl with her settlement. Because Jacob was not her biological father, he was not included in the lawsuit and had no say over what happened with her monies. The financial responsibility was on me as her mother, custodial parent, and payee. And her monies were used for just that. A house was purchased for her that she could literally roll all around. She had all of the home equipment she needed including a lift so she could get down to the lower level of the house with her family and another lift to aide in her getting in and out of her bathtub. She was able to enjoy being in the pool with her siblings and come along on bike rides because she had the necessary equipment. I did not want Baby Girl to miss out on enjoying life simply because of what happened to her. And in a very surprising turn of events, the judge granted me a small settlement as well simply because I didn't ask for one. Fear immediately gripped me. Because I didn't know what Jacob would do or how he would behave to have access to any of the settlement money. In an effort to keep the peace, I gave him half of my settlement. It seemed like it worked for a while, where he just purchased frivolous things like real alligator skinned shoes with the alligator eyes still attached!

Life seemed to be going well for a while, until God revealed Jacob was still cheating and flirting. Why! Why keep doing the same thing that you know will be found out by either of our leaders, or me your wife? I finally learned people who believe that they can't be stopped or corrected will continue to do whatever they want if they think they can get away with it. This was Jacob. In every argument I was the only one who was wrong, could never do right in his eyes, everything was about him, and what mattered to him, not what was best for anyone else. I never really knew what it was called. I just knew he had controlling behaviors, he always wanted people to see him in the best light even though at home he was a completely different person. And then I read about a narcissistic personality. And he fit the description to a tee.

Narcissistic characteristics are:

- A narcissist will get angry when you try to assert your opinion. Who put that thought into your head he would say, as if I was incapable of thinking on my own.
- The narcissist is always right even if their conclusion doesn't make sense. Having overly controlling behavior and spewing grand statements while wanting control, power, and strong desire to lead whether they earn it or not.
- They believe they can become the most famous person in America (assert they have a personal connection to a celebrity), they are well-suited to rule the world, and other delusions of this nature. People call this man an elder and he's never even been ordained past a deacon, and he never corrects his error.
- Narcissists tend to cheat because they get gratification from exploiting others through sexual encounters. Cheating feeds the narcissist's sense of self-validation and power.

- Narcissists share the tendency to exploit others by manipulating their emotions. They will exploit you to gain emotional, sexual, social, and physical validation. One manipulative narcissist tactic is to tell you they have other options, but they still chose you.
- **Narcissists are always right — always. The further you get in your relationship, the veil drops, and they begin to stop saying what they think you want to hear. Then, arguments grow more frequent and more intense.**
- There's no winning the argument because, again, narcissists don't respond to logic. The only time they do is when it serves their purposes. And it leaves you feeling like you can never be heard.
- Narcissists are more likely to wear expensive, flashy clothing, have an organized, neat appearance, requiring a lot of prep time. This man even bought multiple pairs of alligator shoes with real eyes in them.
- In particular, grandiose, and extroverted narcissists don't want to discuss their emotions with you because it puts them in a position of vulnerability and weakens their power over you. If a narcissist does bring up their emotions, it's not genuine. They're using an emotional appeal to get closer to you.
- Their eyes glaze over and become distant when you're talking because they are not listening to you. They're thinking about what they're going to say. To listen to you is to give you the slightest amount of control.

Jacob was all of the above, as well as being financially, and emotionally abusive. I was exhausted to say the least. God, where are you? Why have you not yet rescued me from this torture? Did I want to stay for my kids because I never knew my dad and grew up without a real father figure in my life? Of course, and I wanted the exact the opposite for them. But on the other hand, I was constantly protecting my kids from Jacob; making sure whatever he spewed did not affect the them. I tried to protect their perception about life, especially their understanding of how a man is supposed to treat a woman and how a woman is supposed to treat a man. I wanted to make sure they had healthy self-esteem and egos. I was raising both sons and daughters. The last thing I wanted for them was to think this type of behavior was ok to dish out, or that it was ok to take.

In the long run, the kids knew something was wrong. They felt their own frustrations and doubted their own self-worth when he refused to acknowledge or praise them for their accomplishments, good deeds, or even just for being around. We used to have what we called "family meetings". During these meetings, the kids were allowed to say whatever they wanted to say, however they felt they needed to say it to any other family member without repercussion, as long as they did not curse. Each meeting usually ended with the kids in tears telling their dad what they longed from him. He would be emotional for a short time, but then everything would just go back to normal. No change at all and no resolution for the kids. This was life as we knew it, this was our normal. Me with the kids and their friends for game or movie night and Jacob never wanting to join us.

As time went on, I longed for an answer of how to get out of this marriage. How can God allow me an out biblically? I searched the scriptures high and low and only found passages about how a man can basically throw his wife away just because, but a wife would always be married to her husband, even in death. If a man cheats the wife has no way out, but a man can remarry if his wife cheats and he chooses to divorce her. I wanted out but I did not want to sin against God by divorcing, and I knew I would one day want to remarry. I was so naive to the Word of God and believed what I was told. I believed the Bible favored the male perspective and us women were just their slaves to do with whatever they wanted to. I was truly about to give up on all of it! My marriage, my religion, my belief system, and my faith! What I did know, this was not healthy living. What I didn't know was how to start living.

One particular night as I was ironing Jacob's clothes for the next day, I stopped and looked up and asked God to give me a sign. To tell me what I was supposed to do. The next day I gave Jacob money to pay the cell phone bill. My second oldest daughter had a cell phone but called me from a friend's phone while she was at school telling me her phone wasn't working. I told her not to worry about it and I would take care of it. I never threw Jacob under the bus for not paying it like he was supposed to. Instead, I went to my bedroom with his laptop to login to the cell account to see what was going on. The services were suspended for non-payment just like I thought. While online, I noticed Jacob had his picture on his account, kind of like a profile picture. This was odd to me, but I thought, hey why not add the kids' pictures to my daughter and my accounts since he had a photo on his. I knew a picture of me wouldn't be on his computer, but I figured I might find the kids pictures instead. As I opened up his picture folder, not one photo of the kids was found, but I did find several pictures of the same lady. One where she was in a pink bikini, the other where she was dressed but posing with what appeared to be her young daughter, and another photo of her with a skimpy dress on. She was light skinned with long dark hair. A pretty woman. The memory of Jacob telling me I was the darkest thing he had ever dated ran across my mind at that very moment. I paid the bill, closed the laptop, and looked up to the ceiling and told God, "Thank you". I believed in that moment God gave me my answer. God showed me his behavior would never change, and I was worth more than what I was receiving. Later in the week, I told Jacob I wanted a divorce. He told me it would only be over my dead body and lunged at me while I was getting ready for work. I was in my bathroom, and I almost fell backwards into the tub. The following days he grew more and more angry with me, becoming even nastier with his comments and actions. He even tried to get me to say "divorce" in front of the kids without me knowing they were standing behind him. Anything to make the me the bad guy.

The idea of what he would do to me plagued me daily. All the thoughts of his physical abuse came rushing back like a tidal wave and as the days progressed, I could no longer hold back the tears. I would just burst into tears out of nowhere. One day at work while training a new employee, I could feel my emotions starting to build stronger and stronger. I excused myself to the bathroom, and burst into tears and for the first time, I was unable able to stop. I cried and cried and cried, feeling completely broken and helpless. There was a moment when I had enough strength to open the door to a beautiful soul who was concerned about why I was crying. We went into a separate office, and someone who worked with domestic violence victims came to talk to me. She talked to me about what was going on in my life, and about my options. On the same day we left that office and traveled to the local courthouse and filed for a restraining order. They stayed at the courthouse while the paperwork was being sent to the judge for a decision, and I traveled to the four different schools to pick up my children. My restraining order was approved by the judge that day. My children and I waited around the corner from my home while the deputies escorted him out of the house. This process took over an hour because he was trying to not leave. At this point he wasn't working, again, his name was not on the house, and he had spent all of the money I gave him already, so technically he had nowhere to go. He purposely left his wallet, and other items he later asked his daughter to request from me.

This process was so horrible. The kids had no idea that life was this bad. They wanted to know where their dad was, and they did not understand why I was so sad. I didn't feel relief. I felt like I did when I was a teenager. Looking over my shoulder every moment to see if he was trying to come around. He had his daughter calling me for him, he talked the guard into letting him into the housing community the kids and I lived in although they knew there was a restraining order, and he was not allowed to enter. People at church let him inside the building knowing he was not supposed to be there. Even today, someone still tells him about all the happenings of my life that they see or hear about.

I was already on leave from work and went to counseling three days a week for four straight months while the kids were in school. I should have had the kids go too, but they said they didn't feel the need. I should not have listened, all of us needed help. Soon after, my oldest daughter, my big girl got sick again. Not sure why, she simply caught a cold. We were admitted to the children's hospital in St. Petersburg, Florida. Jacob started working and I had his work number in case of an emergency. I left a message for him to call me about my daughter. We spoke and I told him what was going on. He came to the hospital the next day, but eventually his visits became less and less. My aunt came down from NY to help me with the kids while Baby Girl was in the hospital. I reached out to everyone I knew who could get a prayer through, but no matter who prayed her condition did not improve. As I was getting up from the hospital floor after worshipping God, I had a vision of her funeral. The color of her casket, the video and music that played. That's when I knew I wouldn't be able to pray her through this one. She was admitted on St Patrick's Day in March of 2011 and died just short of a month in April of 2011. I prayed and prayed as I watched her health decline over those twenty-seven days and could not understand why this was happening. My first thought was I caused this to happen. I figured because of my sins, my fleshly ways, my lust problem, my wanting to kiss another man (which I did) and merely thinking about making love to another man before my divorce was over was the reason, I lost her. I did not stay on the wall. I stopped covering her in prayer, I got weak and it was my fault her siblings were broken and hurting.

I desperately needed God to explain to me why He took her. My perfect precious girl who never did anyone harm. Was it really my fault? Did I cause her death? Honestly, I still don't have all the answers and these questions plague me to this day. What I do know is that Baby Girl had her own relationship with God. She had godly desires in her own heart and promises from God that had absolutely nothing to do with me. Then there were promises He made to me as well for my Baby Girl. He promised me that she would dance again, sing again, laugh again, and that she would be happy. And she gets to do all of those things in heaven. Sure, the selfish side of me would love her to be doing those things here, with me and those who truly love her, but God kept His promise. She is getting to do what she loves most. Those thoughts are literally the only reason I have peace about her physically being away from me and in her Heavenly home.

# Chapter 7

# Saying Goodbye

Now it was time that I share with my family what has happened. Jacob finally arrived at the hospital after Baby Girl died. He had ignored all of my phone calls and text messages informing him her condition was going downhill and he needed to make it to the hospital as soon as possible. Not surprisingly, it took him all day and by the time he got there it was too late. He was too busy at the car dealership buying himself a new car (DMV can prove it). My pastors came to the hospital to help me let her go. I had to make the decision to take her off of life support. At this time, she was already brain dead, and her heart was beating so slow. Her heart was not working hard enough to keep her blood flowing, her hands were getting colder, and me keeping her in that state was not doing her any good. After I gave the doctor permission to stop the life support, I was completely numb. Pastor offered to help me with the funeral arrangements. As I prepared to leave, the owner of the funeral home called and said they would come and get her, and we would discuss more in the coming days about my wishes for the service.

It was a very long two-hour drive back to Lakeland, Florida from the children's hospital. I can't recall saying much of anything to Jacob as he drove me home in his new car, except discussing how we would tell the kids. This was the first time I was around him since he was escorted from my home with a restraining order. As I walked in my house the kids saw him walk in behind me and were happy to see their dad. They asked about their sister and wanted to know why I was home without her. We sat them down on the couch, and I proceeded to tell them what happened with their sister and that she would not be coming home. They took it awfully hard. As I watched tears flow down their heart broken little faces and heard the pain in their wailing, I knew I wouldn't be able to handle too much more. I decided to wait to call my family the next morning so I could gain a little more strength after a night of rest. That night was all about my babies and making sure I gave them all the comfort and love they needed. The kids all slept in the bed with me, and we cried ourselves to sleep.

The next day when I woke up, my mom was the first person I called. Her cries were piercing, and her pain was too much to bear on top of my own. I stayed on the phone with her until she was comfortable hanging up. I continued calling my family until eventually my cousin made the remaining calls. Repeating the heartbreaking story was too much for me. Trenton's cousin knew how to get in touch with him and called him on my behalf. Trenton and I spoke briefly, which in normal circumstances would have been a little uncomfortable but this call was dry and straight to the point. After we hung up, Trenton told his mother who called and left a voicemail for me on my answering machine while I was out. Once I got home and listened to the message that night, I decided to call her back the next day. She was a woman who never met her first grandchild, only had an idea that she existed, and was a woman I met for the first time that day over the phone. She felt so much hurt and pain for having missed fifteen years of being in Baby Girl's life and my heart truly went out to her. She immediately offered to help wherever she could. I told her everything was taken care of, so she offered to do the decorations for the repass. Her daughter would help as well, and they would fly down a few days before the funeral.

I was so incredibly numb during the whole planning process. Going to the funeral home and taking photos of my daughter so they could determine how much fluid to drain off of her body. Choosing a cemetery, and then deciding on her burial plot. Finding a company to design her headstone. How did I want the headstone to look? What did I want the words on the headstone to say? Since we had no family in Florida, I had to make arrangements to fly her home. Before her "accident" she was an active member of our first ministry. She sang in the children's choir and helped as an usher. I felt it would be robbery to deny those who really knew her the opportunity to celebrate her life with us. There were a lot of details in getting everything accomplished. This kept my mind busy, and feelings of consuming grief at bay. I comforted those who needed to be comforted and was strong for those who needed my strength. But honestly, it was one of the worst times of my life. From losing my reason for becoming a mother and dealing with a shattered heart to dealing with loneliness and the absence of someone pouring strength back into me. On top of all of this, I had to help my children. Their young hearts had to deal with the recent separation of their parents along with the death of their big sister.

> *I wasn't angry with God. I just could not understand in those moments why He would take her. Was I not a good enough mother? Was it because of whatever she was experiencing while I was working that God said enough is enough? I knew Jacob wasn't taking care of her like he should. Her sister would feed her and act as her caregiver when I had to work. I didn't learn this until many years later. I will never know the answers to these questions.*

> *My prayer life went from consistent praying for her healing and the strength and peace of my other children to absolute silence. I had no idea what to pray. I was no longer sure that my prayers even reached heaven. Was my faith enough for my prayers to come to pass? What I did know was how every single thing heavy on my heart that I petitioned God for in prayer during this time, never came to pass. For example, I prayed*

*that Jacob would become the father his children needed him to be. Yet, at this time, almost twenty-four years later, he is still the same father he has always been. He still causes them pain. They know they can't trust anything he tells them. Furthermore, he continues to place blame on the kids for his own errors instead of taking responsibility for his harmful behaviors. On the other hand, there would be seemingly small, unspoken desires I held in my heart, that would come to pass. I was so confused.*

*In hindsight I have come to a better understanding of what transpired during this season of my life. God has since revealed I was in right standing with Him; my faith was enough; my heart was pure, and He heard me even when I could not pray. Nevertheless, some things didn't change because they had to be a part of not only my testimony, but that of my children's as well.*

*Sometimes we as believers think because we desire something, God is obligated to fulfill the desire. Remember, God's plan and the purpose for your life outweighs what you want or even what your heart desires.*

The next week or so was a blur. We had two homegoing services; one in NY and one in FL. Baby Girl's homegoing service in Florida was truly beautiful. She was laid to rest as the true princess she was, crown and all. She was transported by a white horse drawn carriage with a glass hearse so her beautiful pink and gold casket could be seen by all on the way to her final resting place. Her plot was marked with a tombstone which includes a beautiful photograph of her and two angels praying on each side of her name.

Only one friend, his mother, and his nephew came to our home with food and their condolences. I received very little direct contact from those whom I considered our church family. I can't remember everyone who attended the service, but I can remember not seeing those who claimed to love me and my children. Trenton, his wife, and their children were also at the funeral. At some point during repass I had a meeting with Jacob in my pastor's office. Pastor wanted to know now that this day had come, how we were moving forward. I told Pastor that nothing had changed, my restraining order was still in place, and I was moving forward with the divorce. We left his office and went our separate ways. Jacob, as I would find out later, was not done.

Once the repass was over, I watched as people left the parking lot of the church. Some gave me hugs; some just waved and drove off. Either way, when the kids and I got home, it was just us. No one stayed to be with us. With the phone barely ringing, we were alone again. The kids had me, and I had them, so we dealt with our grief together, as a family. We laughed together. We cried together. We became as close to whole as we could get together.

Jacob was bitter and angry and was doing all he could to make my life miserable. He was sending messages through other people which violated one of the stipulations of the restraining order. "There is to be no third-party contact". He kept trying to come home by telling the police department he left behind important items such as his driver's license and his wallet. We would see his vehicle driving around the area at night, and he would still attend church services.

Eventually, we had someone agree to be our mediator so he could one, get ALL of his belongings, and two, see his children. Due to our violent history, the court mandated him to have supervised visitation with the kids. I never claimed he hurt his children, but this was mandated by the court.

Jacob felt he was losing this battle because things were not going his way. One day he even went on a live radio broadcast and lied to say that the pastor he was in mentorship with and I were having an affair just to drag my name through the mud. He literally was trying to do everything in his power to get back at me for my restraining order and filing for divorce. But he was unable to talk his way out of what he had done. Eventually he just stopped his visitations with the kids. He did not visit, speak with, or see his children for an entire year. The kids were hurt, and they didn't understand the lack of communication. Even still, I avoided speaking negatively to the kids about their dad. I knew one day they would see for themselves who he really was as a person.

After my daughter died, Trenton's mother and I talked every day. She shared intimate revelations about her being a mother, and I shared with her as well. She was a believer, a wife, and a mother. We grew up in the same city and I honestly felt like we could relate to life on many different issues. We became quick friends and talked every day. In some of our conversations, we discussed Trenton, how he's changed over the years due to being in abusive relationships, and the type of father he was to his other children. Eventually, Trenton and I started having regular conversations as well. Yes, he was married, living with his wife and kids. Yes, I was still married, although separated and in the middle of a divorce. We were still married and not at all free to start anything romantic with each other. Over a period of time, our conversations shifted. Initially, the discussions were focused on helping him find the strength to leaving an abusive relationship. Then we began to discuss the possibility of him moving to Florida to be with me; which is exactly what happened.

Perhaps it was the death of the child we shared. Perhaps it was misdirected grief, I'm not completely certain. What I knew is that we had a spiritual connection so strong that when he was in the building, I could feel his presence without actually seeing him *(that would be a soul tie people, didn't realize it wasn't broken until after that)*. I knew that when I looked into his eyes or even saw his face, I saw my baby girl, and that was all I needed at the time. It did not matter to me that he would come with nothing, or that he had other children that needed him. Back then, I could not see how introducing what would be a stranger to my children could potentially affect them. I trusted the person I used to know. I was broken and hurting and honestly didn't see past my own hurt. Later

I would live to realize this would be the absolute worst decision I would ever make in my life!

# Chapter 8

# Is This One Prince Charming? I Know He's No Boaz ☹

Before Trenton moved to Florida I prayed daily for direction and wisdom while trying to push through brokenness, pain, and confusion. The goal was for him to have his own place while we worked out our individual issues. To not live together and to not start anything romantic until it was safe to do so. We made appointments with realtors and management companies to look at apartments, and we also made many phone calls trying to find a place for him without any success. As part of the agreement with Jacob, the children and I would live in the house until my youngest turned eighteen-years old, after which we would share ownership of the house. But Jacob assumed Trenton was already living in the house, changed his promise in front of the judge and we then had to sell the house as part of the divorce settlement. This meant, while I was looking for a new place, Trenton was looking for a permanent place. We decided to combine our efforts and bought a home together.

Jacob saw Trenton at church with me one day and was furious. Jacob never liked Trenton and never wanted him in Baby Girl's life. Apparently, Jacob had exchanged phone numbers with Trenton's wife during my daughter's funeral and they had kept in touch since that time. Jacob decided to call and inform her where her husband had disappeared. Jacob also told her my address, description of the house, along with the make, model, color, and license plate number of my vehicle. In the beginning, she started calling my pastor in hopes that he could convince Trenton to return home. One day, my pastor had over twenty voice messages from her and her children. When she finally spoke with the pastor, she mentioned the information Jacob had given to her. My pastor made sure to relay this to me so that I was aware.

As time progressed, we began working on opening a barbershop for Trenton so he could have his own steady source of income. One day while he was at work, he made a run to a nearby store for supplies. While in the store, he bumped into his wife! She was supposed to be in a whole other state with their children. She flew out the back door of the store. Trenton had previously applied for a restraining order against her due to her shooting his car when he attempted to spend time with his kids. In addition, she already had pending DCF charges, was on felony probation for arson, and was not allowed to leave her state due to her violent history. Unfortunately, by the time they finally arrived, the authorities were unable to find her. It was around this same time she started calling the local sheriff's office not knowing I was employed there. One day when covering a lunch, I intercepted her phone call. She was trying to get Trenton arrested by telling them he had criminal charges pending in another state. After following up on her allegations, the authorities figured out she was lying.

Based on their violent past, Trenton indeed had been through a lot like his mother said. He was no longer the same man I met all those years ago. He was broken and he was hurt. And with that he treated me like he had treated so many others. He flirted with other women, he cheated with other women, and before it was over, used me for everything he could take me for. The money left over from the settlement had been split during my divorce since Jacob adopted Baby Girl, but my remaining funds seemed to be dwindling faster than I was spending. I had always been good with money and am a saver at heart. And honestly, I just didn't see it until it was too late. I even went as far as having a meeting with my banker to figure out where this slow leak of funds was coming from. Whenever I asked Trenton about where the missing money was, he never knew and said it was probably identity theft. I eventually filed a police report to try to figure it all out. Before long, we were arguing every day. We argued about his spending and where all the money was going. We argued about his behavior inside and outside of the house. All of the morals and values I tried instilling in my children went out of the door when they watched his behavior. At first everything was fine (like it usually is). He talked to the kids like a father figure, and by not having one they seemed to soak it up. It made my heart happy to see them genuinely developing a relationship with a man who treated them like his children. That was until it all stopped. Underneath it all, Trenton didn't truly want to be a father to my kids, his kids, or anyone else's kids. What he wanted was to live a single life and have a wife. At the end of the day, you can't have your cake and eat it too. But he sure did try!

It's Sunday July 15, 2012. Trenton and I had been arguing so much leading up to this day. About finances, about his role in the house, his treatment of my children. There was literally nothing that was going right. He claimed he wanted to do right, and he loved God, but his actions said the exact opposite. After leaving church around 9:15p.m., that night, I decided to stop at a gas station and pick up some juice for the house. Because we drove separate cars, I called Trenton to see if he wanted anything. My kids were with their dad, and I was driving home alone. When I pulled into my driveway and drove up to the garage door, I saw the broken, brown wooden chair that seemed to have appeared out of nowhere a few days ago. No one seemed to know who it belonged to or where it came from. This was just one of the odd things that had gone on around the house leading up to that night. I reached up and pushed the button on the garage door opener to open the garage so I could pull in. My mind was so consumed with that prayer from my pastor's wife earlier that night. She prayed for me like never before. I felt as if she was covering me, but from what? After her prayer and many tears, I felt I knew what I had to do next. I needed to separate from Trenton. I knew he wasn't happy. He knew I wasn't happy, and the kids were not happy either. It was time that I started making plans. I had so much on my mind, I honestly didn't notice if anything was out of order when I got home. I got out of my SUV with the bag from the store and my purse in hand, closed the car door behind me and walked toward the door to the house as I heard the car lock. I opened the house door, which was not locked, and I turned to close it and as I turned forward, I was almost face to face with what appeared to be a dark, slender, female figure, wearing some kind of hat. It was dark in the house, but I could make out the shape of the person standing in front of me from the streetlights that illuminated from the dining room windows. POW! She was holding a gun and shot me in my chest. "Why would you. . ." Her aim lowered while I was talking and POW again! This time, she shot me in the leg. I purposely fell backward to fall on the stairs that were behind me. She then grabbed my feet and drug me down the hall into the formal living room which was behind the kitchen. A huge wall separated the two rooms and because of the house floorplan, you couldn't even see the room unless you actually entered it. No one would know I was there until they walked into the room. She drug me so my feet were facing the door leading to the backyard. Then she walked away. I heard her walking on the hardwood floor back to where I dropped my shopping bag and purse. Then I heard her pick up whatever fell and walk back down to me. My breathing was quicker, but the only thing I was thinking of was don't breathe…don't breathe. Every time she was near me, she would stand close. There was absolutely no sound in the house. She was very quiet. I believe she was trying to see if I was still alive. I held my breath anytime she was close so she would believe I was dead.

I prayed to myself asking God what should I do? What should I do? When she finally stopped walking near me, I assume she got into position because as soon as Trenton came walking through the front door, he turned on the light, and POW! She shot him in the back. He turned around to see her face and yelled something I couldn't make out along with the phrase, "Shot me!" The next thing I heard was two sets of shoes running in different directions and two doors slamming shut. No one knew I was even home. My car was in a closed garage. My body was lying in a room no one could see.

Knowing the house was empty, I immediately reached up behind me and locked the back door then I crawled to the front door and locked that too. I then attempted to stand, but I just couldn't. I crawled back down the hallway into my bedroom where I knew there was a house phone. When I didn't find it, I crawled back down the hall to the kitchen to get the phone from there. No house phone there either. Then I heard a phone ring. I crawled back down the hallway again to try and locate this phone. As I crawled around the bed and reached the side closest to the window, I grabbed my chest. Knowing I was shot there, but when I looked down at my hand, I could not see any blood. I saw no blood with all the crawling back and forth I did, but I knew I had been shot. I wasn't in any pain, but I felt weaker than I had ever felt before in my life. At some point, I passed out on the side of my bed. I heard a man with a loud voice saying, "Come out with your hands up!" I just raised my hand over the bed and said, "Help I'm here! I need help!" I had no strength. This was an hour after EMS arrived to take Trenton to the hospital after neighbors had called 911.

As soon as I saw the police, I told them everything that happened and who did it. I repeated my story until I was in the ambulance. The EMT's pulled me up, one standing on each side of me, had me walk from the back entrance where my vehicle was parked around the front of my house to the ambulance that was parked in front of the neighbor's house. At that point I couldn't walk anymore, and they put me on the stretcher and into the ambulance. As I lay on the stretcher, I remember them trying to take off my shirt and had me roll over. They told me to grab a bar that was to my right with my left hand. I pulled it, turned over, and that was the last I remembered until I woke up a week later in the hospital.

# Chapter 9

# July 2012

I was told when I arrived in the ER, I gave them my pastors name and phone number and told them to call him. Pastor woke up his son and they drove as fast as they could to the hospital. My first cousin was my health proxy, so her name and phone number were already in the hospital records. When my family got the call early that next morning, they flew down immediately and were at the hospital by evening. One of the deputies on duty was a member of our church and was able to get my pastor as close to the operating room doors as he could. While there, Pastor saw my surgeon praying before he began operating on me. He too went into immediate prayer while I was in surgery; anointing the operating room doors. Even after the surgery, they did not think I was going to make it due to the extreme damage I had and the amount of blood I lost.

Jacob had the kids with him. While with him, my daughter saw a post by my pastor's son asking for prayer because his spiritual sister and brother were in an accident. After my daughter "liked" his post, she received a call from him asking how I was doing. When she didn't understand the question, he told her it was me and Trenton that were shot. She instantly broke down into tears in the corner of her bedroom. When Jacob heard her crying, he headed into her room. Without asking what was wrong, or why she was crying, he took her phone, walked out, and closed the door behind him. When recounting her experience that same night, she mentioned that prior to seeing the post from the pastor's son, she heard Jacob on the phone while pacing back and forth saying, "They're coming for me, they're coming for me". At the time, she didn't know what he was talking about. She also mentioned she saw a woman's name on Jacob's phone which was the same name as Trenton's ex-wife.

The deputies called Jacob to have him bring the kids to the hospital to see me before it was too late, but he refused. The sheriff's office deputies brought my children to the hospital because they knew how much they meant to me. My children were on a sports team that many from the sheriff's office were a part. They were very familiar with my children outside of my career there.

After Jacob refused, sheriff's office deputies volunteered to pick-up the kids and bring them back to the hospital. Continuing to be difficult, he gave them a fake address which further delayed my children getting to me. Eventually they found my daughter's phone number and called her. After she was able to get her phone back, they had to give her instructions to sneak and find the correct address. They then instructed her on what to do once they arrived. They would knock on the door and she was to open it and simply stand aside so they could do their job. Once the kids finally arrived at the hospital, the sheriff's office sergeant was the first one to tell my boys what happened. This was quite a traumatic experience for them. So much so, that my oldest son's reaction when he heard what happened to me was punching a hole in the chapel wall.

Outside the hospital, the deputies had found and arrested the ex-wife and started their investigation. They found many clues implicating Jacob to the crime. Certainly, the fact that he was in court with his lawyer very early the next morning attempting to get full custody of my children was a red flag. We already shared joint custody, so there was no real point for this new filing. My guess was he knew anything I had would be left to my children. That's the only reason I could imagine he would be filing for full custody. To this day, I still don't know the real reason. During the investigation his cell phone, laptop, iPad, printer, and any other electronic device he owned was confiscated for evidence. Unsurprisingly, he refused to give them the password to his cell phone. When they finally were able to access his data by court orders, the evidence they needed was gone. They knew that Jacob and the ex-wife had been communicating since Baby Girl's funeral. They knew that Jacob and the ex-wife were communicating while she was waiting in my house that night, and they also knew that Jacob had everything to do with my shooting. Yet, all of this was meaningless because they did not have enough concrete evidence to charge him with anything. Furthermore, when Trenton's ex-wife had the opportunity to tell the truth, she never said a thing. She didn't explain anything that happened. She never explained why. She never said who, or how she acquired the key to my home, and she never said who helped her plan the shooting. The only general statement she would make was to ask Jacob; he knew all about it.

By the end of the investigation and trial, the ex-wife had received a sentence of 15 to 30 years for shooting us both. They are consecutive years, which means she would have to serve them back to back not altogether. If she happens to be released early for good behavior, she would have served a minimum of 30-years, and by then would be somewhere in her 60's. Upon release, she will be extradited to her home state to face her pending charges there.

After having lived with Trenton and seeing firsthand how someone can be good to him and he turn on you, I am not angry with his ex-wife. I understand where she may have been coming from. Feeling like she's due. Feeling like how dare you go off and live this great life after you treated me the way you did. So, I get it. From what I heard about her; she was a good woman with a great future in nursing before getting with Trenton. I cannot excuse her actions, but I am no longer mad at her because of them.

Recovery after my shooting was long and it was hard. I ended up losing a kidney, my spleen, my gallbladder, some of my pancreas, part of a lung, intestines, stomach, and liver. I lost a lot of blood and had multiple transfusions in attempts to keep me stable. In the process, I also ended up with brain damage due to a lack of oxygen to the brain. I was unable to talk due to a machine that was forcing air into my lungs and was only able to communicate by writing the best I could. After waking up a week later I finally saw my children. I was overwhelmed with emotion when seeing them after such a traumatic ordeal. I don't remember them crying when they saw me, but I know it was overwhelming for them as well. Thankfully, my family showed up in full force and took my children with them. Once they all left the hospital, my family members tried their best to find ways to help my children get back to some level of normalcy.

This was no easy journey. I was fighting with major PTSD and on heavy pain medications. I suffered from horrible hallucinations. When I would hear the beeping from the different hospital machines, I thought it was the elevator arriving on my floor with the ex-wife exiting the elevator to finish the job. At other times I could hear the helicopter and thought it was landing over my hospital room and she was coming through the ceiling vent to kill me. They were not all full of fear and death. In one vision I was in all white and holding the hand of a little person dressed in all white, with a man dressed in all white as well. I could not see who they were, but I felt like maybe it was a family that I was supposed to have been a part of. I thought perhaps that was God's plan for me, not this.

After learning how to sit up I had to learn to walk again, my oldest son would walk with me up and down the hallway to help me regain my strength. I was finally able to leave the hospital and go home. Because of the internal damage to my organs, I was unable to really eat. I was only able to eat .5g of fat per meal and lost a lot of weight. I only weighed about 130lbs to begin with. I went down to a size double zero and that was still baggy on me. I also lost my hair. When it did eventually grow back, it was much thinner than my previous hair, and some areas didn't grow back at all. Recovery was grueling but was in no comparison to what Jacob was putting me through to get my kids back. When he filed for full custody, the judge granted him temporary custody until I was able to take care of them. His lawyer was ruthless. Nevertheless, in the end God allowed my babies to come home and we were finally back together.

The investigation you ask. Well, let's just say it never went anywhere. No additional charges were ever filed. Jacob walked away scot-free. Trenton and I were married because I wanted to do things right before God. The union did not last long. We divorced after all my money, my daughter's money, was gone. Later my family filled me in on some of what went on during my weeklong coma. This is some of what was recounted to me:

On the morning of Monday July 16th, my cousin missed a call from Jacob at 5:30 a.m. She called him back around 8:00 a.m. He then told her I had been shot and was in the hospital. She called her mom and decided to fly to Florida. She tried getting information from the hospital about my condition, but they didn't provide it over the phone. Finding my siblings was difficult, so it took them longer to finally make the plane reservations. When they arrived later that evening they headed straight to the hospital. They were sent to an ICU waiting room and the surgeon who performed my first surgery came to see them. The surgeon said I barely made it through the first surgery and described in detail all of my injuries. He told them I had been shot three times *(really only two)* and the locations of the bullet wounds. He told my family the bullet went through my breast destroyed my kidney, hit my spleen and pancreas. Injuries to my stomach and other organs were also discussed. During the operation my spleen and 70% of my pancreas had to be removed. There were also some repairs to my stomach. I would require a second surgery the following Wednesday.

After the first surgery, my cousin came back to see me and said I was hooked up to a ventilator, in and out of consciousness and very scared. She didn't know what was wrong with me, but they told her I lost a lot of blood. The police came to speak with her and told her that they had not caught the female suspect, but they knew she was on her way back to her home state. At some point the police told my cousin the suspect had been apprehended and they were bringing her back to Florida to face the charges. My family stayed overnight at the hospital and rotated shifts.

Another person gave this account:

My aunt fought to gain temporary custody of my kids. At some point she had a talk with my daughter. At that time, my daughter said her father and this woman had been talking a lot. She would overhear them talking on the phone when she was visiting with him. She said the Saturday evening before I was shot, he was talking to this woman on the phone. This conversation was relayed to the police who replied by saying they were already investigating Jacob.

The days and weeks leading up to my shooting, there were very strange conversations being had with my daughter and Jacob. He was continuously asking what Trenton and I were up to? What our schedules were like? What time we were home, and other odd questions. I can recall one day I heard my daughter answer question after question. After I asked who she was speaking with, she put the phone on speaker, and I heard the questions Jacob was asking her. I interrupted the conversation and told him to not ask her any questions about me and that any information about me was none of his business. Trenton also had a separate run in with Jacob about questioning my daughter about his whereabouts. Trenton told

Jacob that if he wanted to know something to come to him directly and not use a child to get information. Little did we know the reason he was asking all those questions.

One final note of irony. Just hours before trying to gain full custody of my children believing my death was imminent, leaving him to benefit from whatever was left to my children; he called MY family to tell them I had been shot. This was such a blatant demonstration of narcissistic behavior. Let me be the one to call the family so they won't think I had anything to do with the shooting and be fooled into believing that I care. For anyone who asked Jacob how I was doing his response and behavior was as if he was there, in the hospital with access to information about my recovery. When, in reality he was being investigated for his role in the crime and could be nowhere near me or my family. He was only allowed at the hospital doors to drop off or pick up my children.

*Chapter 10*

# Pieces of Evidence: This is a true story after all!

IN THE CIRCUIT/COUNTY COURT OF THE TENTH JUDICIAL
CIRCUIT IN AND FOR POLK COUNTY, FLORIDA

AGENCY #
OBTS #
BOOKING #
CASE #

**ARREST WARRANT**

IN THE NAME OF THE STATE OF FLORIDA:

TO: All and singular, the sheriff's of Florida and other authorized officers.

WHEREAS the Court has found probable cause from the sworn complaint affidavit or other testimony under oath to believe that the person named below committed:

1. ATTEMPTED MURDER 1ST DEGREE - 2 COUNTS   F.S.782.04(1A1)   F/C
2. ARMED BURGLARY OF DWELLING-FIREARM   F.S.810.02(2B)   F/1
3. POSSESSION FIREARM OR CONCEALED WEAPON BY CONVICTED FELON
   F.S.790.23(1A)   F/2
4. POSSESSION OF AMMUNITION BY CONVICTED FELON   F.S.790.23   F/2

YOU ARE HEREBY COMMANDED to arrest, instanter, the person named below for the crime(s) named above to be brought before the Court and dealt with according to the law.

Defendant
Address
DOB
Social Se
Place of
                                                                          Alias
Marital Status UNK    Occupation UNK         Employer UNK
Bail is set at:  1.  NO BOND EACH - 2 COUNTS
                 2.  NO BOND UNTIL FAH
                 3.  $5,000 CASH OR SURETY
                 4.  $5,000 CASH OR SURETY

, returned on demand.

GIVEN UNDER MY HAND AND SEAL THIS 16 DAY OF July, 2012

JUDGE

Janice Lucas

**STATEMENT OF FACTS CONSTITUTING PROBABLE CAUSE**
Case Number: ▓

On 07/15/2012 at approximately 2237 hours, the Polk County Sheriff's Office was notified of a shooting and responded to the residence located at ▓, Lakeland, FL. While landline with the reportee, ▓ advised dispatchers that his ex-wife, later identified as ▓ ct) shot him. It was further learned that victim ▓ advised dispatchers he ran outside the residence and believed the suspect was still inside his residence.

Upon arrival to the gated community in which the victim resides, deputies observed victim ▓ exiting the subdivision. Upon contact with Victim ▓ deputies learned he was shot in his back. Victim ▓ explained that he and Victim Lucas live together in the residence and they arrived home separately from church. Victim ▓ said he entered through the front door of the residence and as he walked toward the kitchen he was shot in the back by his ex-wife, whom he positively identified as the suspect.

Additional deputies arrived to the area and entry was made into the victims' residence. A search of the residence revealed the suspect was no longer inside. Victim Lucas was located in the master bedroom on the south side of the bed. Victim Lucas advised deputies she had been shot multiple times. Both victims were transported by ambulance to Lakeland Regional Medical Center where they underwent surgery to treat their injuries.

Detectives contacted victim ▓ fter surgery. Victim ▓ stated he walked into his home via the front door and as he was approaching the kitchen he was shot from behind. Victim ▓ stated he turned around and observed his ex-wife ▓ whom he positively identified as the suspect. Victim ▓ stated the suspect then fired at least one more round at him and he fled the residence through the garage.

On July 16, 2012 an arrest warrant was issued for ▓ on charges of Attempted First Degree Murder (2 counts), Armed Burglary, Possession of Firearm by Convicted Felon and Possession of Ammunition by Convicted Felon. Approximately eleven hours after the incident, ▓ was arrested on the warrant in ▓

During a post-Miranda sworn recorded interview with ▓ she implicated ▓, the ex-husband of Victim Lucas, as having involvement in the incident. ▓ advised ▓ is upset with Janice Lucas over a recent ▓ wrongful death settlement involving their deceased child. ▓ advised ▓ has been plotting the murder of Janice Lucas in order to have access to Lucas' portion of the malpractice settlement through the remaining three children they have in common. ▓ repeatedly stated that ▓ "knows everything" and she repeatedly encouraged detectives to "check his cell phone records".

During an interview with ▓, conducted in the presence of his attorney, ▓ confirmed that he is upset with Lucas over the time he lost with their deceased child before the child's death. ▓ denied knowledge or involvement in the shooting. ▓ advised that his cellular phone number is ▓ with service supplied by AT&T. ▓ stated he was at his residence at ▓ Florida at the time of the shooting. ▓ stated that he had not spoken with ▓ in several months.

Filed Polk County Clerk of Court 2013-02-15 09:27

▓ and ▓ cell phone records were reviewed after investigative subpoenas were obtained. Multiple text messages were sent and received between ▓ and ▓ phones throughout the day and less than an hour before the shooting on July 15, 2012.

On July 25, 2012, a search warrant was obtained in Osceola County for ▓ residence. Such search warrant was executed on July 25, 2012 at ▓ residence located at ▓ Found within ▓ residence, and collected as evidence, were the following items:

# How Did I Get Here? A Story of God's Grace

## The Ledger

Couple shot in their home; suspect found - News - The Ledger -

**Couple shot in their home; suspect found By ELVIA MALAGON / Ledger Media Group**

LAKELAND - As Janice Lucas arrived home from church Sunday evening, she saw what looked like a shadow in the hallway of her home.

Lucas, 35, told deputies she was shot five times and was dragged into a bedroom in her home at ▮▮▮▮▮▮▮▮▮ in Lakeland, Polk County Sheriff Grady Judd said. She was shot in the chest, abdomen, legs, and arm. Lucas told deputies she pretended to be dead as she heard the shooter reloading the firearm.

About 20 minutes later, she told deputies she heard another round of shots.

Her fiancé, ▮▮▮▮▮▮▮▮▮ arrived home from church when he was shot twice at about 10:30 p.m., Judd said.

He managed to get out of the house and to ask for help.

Deputies arrested ▮▮▮ estranged wife, ▮▮▮▮▮▮▮▮▮, Monday morning at her Kinsey, Ala., home. She faces charges of two counts of attempted first-degree murder,

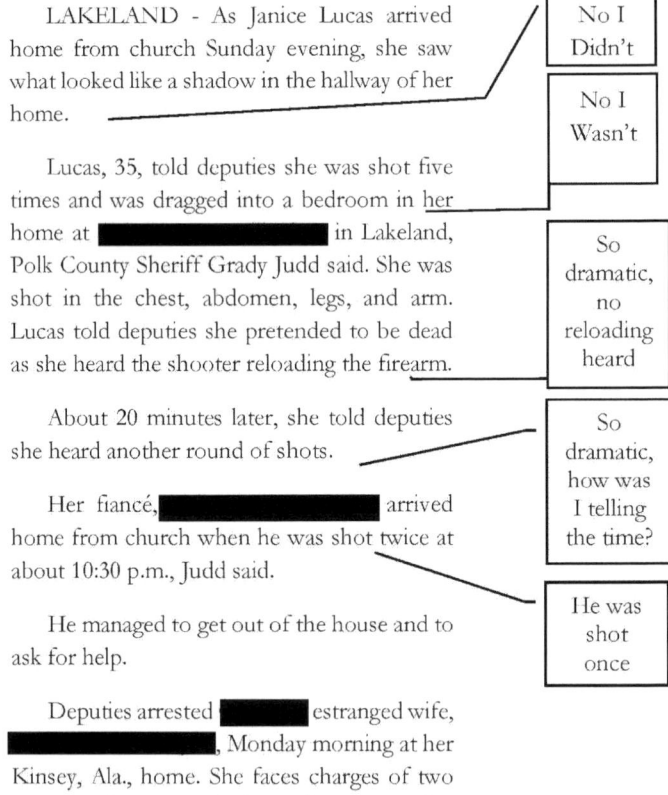

- No I Didn't
- No I Wasn't
- So dramatic, no reloading heard
- So dramatic, how was I telling the time?
- He was shot once

armed burglary, possession of a firearm by a convicted felon and possession of ammunition by a convicted felon.

Lucas is in very critical condition and ▓▓▓ is in stable condition at Lakeland Regional Medical Center, deputies said. The two identified ▓▓▓ as the shooter.

Judd said ▓▓▓ parked her vehicle Sunday at a nearby subdivision and then broke into the couple's home.

Deputies said ▓▓▓ had prior arrests in Alabama, including two charges of domestic violence.

On Monday, deputies sorted through the intertwined lives of the three people involved in the shooting.

> They tried

Lucas and ▓▓▓ first crossed paths more than a decade ago in Rochester, N.Y., when they had a daughter together, Judd said. The two went their separate ways and married other people.

> So far so good…

In January 2002, ▓▓▓ and ▓▓▓ married and had three children together, according to court records.

Lucas and ▓▓▓ rekindled their relationship recently just before the death of their daughter. It was unclear Monday how their daughter died.

> Rekindling didn't happen until months after baby girl passed away.

# How Did I Get Here? A Story of God's Grace

Lucas divorced her husband and ▮ was in the process of divorcing ▮ ▮ works at a barbershop in Haines City and Lucas worked in a civilian position at the Polk County Sheriff's Office.

After the death of her daughter, Lucas and her former husband received a large settlement check from a hospital, Judd said.

Detectives suspect that money is one of the motives for the shooting.

| My divorce was almost a year prior. Trenton owned the shop. |
|---|

| My daughter and I received that settlement 4 years prior, Jacob was not a part of it. |
|---|

Oh, and please whatever you do, don't take the news at face value! The story they reported was twisted. From my experience, it's the story they want, not necessarily the truth in the story.

There were so many news articles about the incident. Ironically, I was never interviewed by anyone. I was too busy fighting for my life, not giving press releases. While still in the hospital, I remember waking up in the middle of the night and overheard a nurse talking about what she read. She then stated that I deserved what I got. Our neighbors stopped talking to us and the kids were no longer allowed to play with their children. Our lives were turned upside down because of the extensive coverage and how the story was reported.

## Chapter 11

# What Does It All Mean? Lessons Learned!

Did I mess up during these years? You better believe it! Did I regret it each time? Sure did! Did I sit back and allow God to heal my brokenness so it would be easier to resist my flesh and everything my flesh wanted? Nope! That only came years later. Even after all you just read in experiencing failed relationship after failed relationship, I did not learn to make better decisions overnight. It took me seeking God about what was broken in me and what needed to be fixed. My self-esteem was broken. All I ever heard was how worthless I was, and how I could never do anything right from the men I loved. My heart was broken. My purpose was broken and unknown, and I still needed healing from all of my childhood trauma. What was it about me that continued to attract that same kind of personality and behavior?

Once God revealed to me it was my brokenness and my unquenchable desire to be loved and accepted, I had to change my mindset and thought process about what behavior and treatment was acceptable in my life. God revealed that I was worth more than I was used to settling for, (Proverbs 31:10 "Who can find a virtuous woman? For her price is far above rubies"). He accepts me, faults and all and he sees deeper than what man sees in me (Daniel 2:22 "He reveals deep and hidden things; He knows what lies in darkness, and light dwells within Him"). His love for me runs deeper than any love I've experienced. (John :16 "For God so loved the World He gave His only begotten son".) I don't love any person on this earth more than I love my children, and to try to think of how difficult it would be to sacrifice one of my children for another person is imaginable. It was time that I do the work and allow God to break me, gracefully. To rebuild me in Him. It was not a feel-good process. I spent nights crying in prayer because of all the things I had done and the disappointment I know I caused my heavenly Father. I would pray my sins didn't negatively impact my children, and for God to spare them. I prayed, fasted, and consecrated myself before God and asked to be made over, to be made new. I asked God to break every spiritual soul tie that was connected to me, I asked God to heal the brokenness so I could be whole in Him, I prayed that God would send people in my life who were truly meant to be there. And I asked God to give me peace about not knowing my dad. I know that I look like him, and there are times I think about who he may have been. But now I have peace about not knowing him (Philippians 4:6 "And the peace that surpasses all understanding will guard your hearts and minds in Jesus Christ"). I have peace knowing that I am fearfully and wonderfully made (Psalms 139:14 "I will praise thee; for I am fearfully and wonderfully made..."). I was created with great reverence, heart-felt intention, and respect to be unique and set apart. The Word of God, much time in prayer, counseling, life coach sessions, and purposely involving myself in anything that could help my mindset change is how I slowly became a better me. I had to see the ugly, nasty, disgusting parts of me to know that they existed, but to also know that it was not meant to be a part of me. By God's grace, I am better today than I was a year ago, and tomorrow I will be better than I am today.

So, what was it that I learned from all of this? One of the biggest lessons I learned through these years and all of these situations is the importance of praying BEFORE making decisions. I'm not going to say that I didn't pray before I made decision to be in the relationships I was in, but what I didn't do was wait on God to reply. If I had waited on God, I could have avoided abuse, heartache, being taken advantage of, and not only for myself but also for my children.

God also revealed I had unforgiveness in my heart towards anyone including my mother who made me feel less than or caused any kind of pain in my life. But I had to forgive them, and I had to forgive myself. I had to take responsibility for the parts that I played. And forgive myself for allowing things to happen because of the bad choices I made. Because the longer I beat myself up, the longer it was going to take to truly move forward in peace, in joy, and in the life God had planned for me. I had to forgive.

Another lesson I learned was the importance of waiting after praying. I feel like sometimes we are in such a hurry to do and or be what we believe God wants us to do or to be, but we have to just stand and wait on the timing of God. We are to be patient in well doing and stand strong on the Word that God spoke to you directly! Sometimes prayers can be answered in the form of prophesy, just remember prophesy is supposed to be God confirming to you through someone what God spoke to you already.

You should never allow anyone to make you feel less than. The majority of my adult life I felt I was dumb, stupid, worthless, not a woman of God, that I had no faith, and I had no power because of what the men in my life would tell me. But I had to come to the realization that those were just lies from the father of lies! That isn't how God sees me.

We are made in the likeness and image of God which means when you were created it was not a mistake. You were made to be the perfect you that you are. Please know your worth! Know that you are worthy of love, worthy of adoration, worthy of transparency, worthy of acceptance, worthy of the joy and peace that comes from God! If he/she does not love you the way you need to be loved, don't move forward unless God Himself speaks to you regarding that person being in your life. Whatever God blesses you with won't be a burden. I'm not saying every relationship will be easy, there will be ups and downs and that's normal. But if there are more downs than ups, and if those downs make you feel like you're not worth living, please discuss it with someone you trust. That relationship isn't building you up, its tearing you down and you have to know that is not God's will for your life!

Allow God to give you a spirit of discernment. Your discernment is key! Hearing the voice of God and trusting Him to lead and guide your decisions can be the difference between a life and death situation without you knowing.

Stay in the will of God. Do your best to push through and push past your feelings and emotions when you don't want to be bothered. Remember that there is no good thing in our flesh and feelings and emotions are flesh.

Know that if you reach out to others, they will reach back. No matter if you feel like you don't want to bother anyone, reach out anyway. You are never really alone. God will bring people into your life that you can trust and who will uplift and encourage you when you need it most. If you allow Him to, God can cultivate an entire community of people who will love you for who you are, and you will love them back.

Bad things will happen in this life no matter what kind of great person you try to be and no matter how many mistakes you avoid. The truth of the matter is; you don't have to do anything wrong for bad things to happen. Take for example the biblical story of Job. He lived an entire life that was pleasing to God, yet God allowed bad things to happen to him. Despite the pain he must have felt, despite the anguish and agony that consumed his life, the one thing that Job did was continue to trust God. That does not mean he avoided complaining, because in his lowest moments he did complain. Ultimately, he pulled himself together and praised and trusted God in spite of what was before him (This story can be found in the bible, book of Job). This was a critical lesson for me. No matter how low my life got, I knew God was giving me the strength to get through. He was letting me know He still had my back despite my past, despite my mistakes, despite my complaining. God still loved me enough to show me He still has my back and He has yours too!

Maintaining your peace needs to be one of the essential and crucial parts of your life. When you allow others to disturb your peace, you begin living a stressful life, a life full of bitterness and anger can overtake you. Your peace is important, and you need to treat it that way. Anything or anyone that comes against your peace needs to be removed from your life. Now I'm not telling you to completely cut loved ones out of your life, but sometimes those jokers need to be fed with a long-handled spoon! You should do whatever you need to do to ensure when you wake up each morning the only goal you have is to be in the will of God. Let God show you how to protect your peace at all costs.

One last thing that I learned was to stop putting myself on the back burner and serving everyone else first. If you're not in a good headspace, you're stressed out, you're overworked, your mind is in a million different places, and your concentration is off. How can you really give 100% of your efforts to what matters to you most if you are mentally, physically, and spiritually exhausted? You have to take time out for yourself. Whether it is once a month, or just an hour, do something just for you, something that brings you peace, that allows you to just be you. It could be a simple drive by yourself or with friends, maybe a beach day, or even getting a hotel for one and sleeping all day! Find whatever you need to regroup and re-strengthen your thoughts, your body, and your spirit so when you get back to reality, you are fully prepared to give as much of yourself that you need to give. Put yourself first and do so without any regret.

It was the grace of God I was not aborted in my mother's womb. It was the grace of God I was kept from being infected by AIDS or HIV when I was a lost young girl full of brokenness and pain. It was the grace of God that prevented the car from running me over when I was walking with my daughters. It was the grace of God which kept me during 15-years of the worst abuse of my life. It was the grace of God that kept my mind after my daughter and mother died only 8-months apart. It was truly God's grace that allowed me to forgive my mother for all the damage done in my childhood long before she died. It was the grace of God that kept me during and after my shooting; and it is the Grace of God that continues to keep me daily!

Your peace and your happiness is not a goal, it is a requirement. God is Faithful. God is Able. God is Love. You've Got This. Be Blessed.

Made in the USA
Columbia, SC
31 October 2021